Religion, Theology,
and American Public Life

SUNY Series in Religious Studies
Harold Coward, Editor

Religion, Theology, and American Public Life

Linell Elizabeth Cady

State University of New York Press

Published by
State University of New York Press, Albany

© 1993 State University of New York

For information, address State University of New York
Press, State University Plaza, Albany, N.Y., 12246

Production by Diane Ganeles
Marketing by Bernadette LaManna

Library of Congress Cataloging-in-Publication Data

Cady, Linell Elizabeth, 1952–
    Religion, theology, and American public life / Linell Elizabeth
Cady.
        p.   cm. — (SUNY series in religious studies)
    ISBN 0-7914-1303-9 (hard : alk. paper). — ISBN 0-7914-1304-7
(pbk. : alk. paper)
    1. United States—Religion. 2. Religion and sociology—United
States. 3. Theology—Methodology.   I. Title. II. Series.
    BL2525.C33   1993
230'.0973—dc20   92-3097
                                                                          CIP

10 9 8 7 6 5 4 3 2 1

For my parents
Elizabeth A. Cady
and
George L. Cady

Contents

Preface

This book is as much a book on theology as it is one of theology. In large part it reflects my effort to work out a satisfactory identity as a theologian within the context of a religious studies department of a large public university. This location has proved both challenging and fruitful, although not always in equal measures. From my colleagues I have certainly learned a great deal about religion which I now think is far more relevant to theology than I had once presumed. At the same time I have had to deal with the suspicions and skepticism of some colleagues regarding the academic merit of the genre of theology. And unlike theologians situated within exclusively graduate institutions, this location has forced me to confront the widespread indifference of many undergraduate students who, lacking any professional interest or stake in the field, quickly dismiss it as academic obfuscation with little relevance beyond itself.

But perspectives beyond the university have also affected me as well. With many others I have become increasingly aware of and disturbed by the cultural marginalization of the academic enterprise of theology. This general observation has often been corroborated for me in conversations with family, friends, and acquaintances who in one way or another give voice to the failure of theology to have much impact beyond its professional boundaries.

The audience that existed in my mind's eye as I wrote, then, was diverse, variously including external critics, fellow theologians, and bored students. I soon realized, however, that these voices were not simply "out there." They had come to constitute me as well, demanding some interpretive resolution to their oftentimes unsettling perspectives. This work, then, reflects my effort to think through the nature of theology against the backdrop of these shifting points of view to chart a direction for the future of the genre as much for myself as for others.

"Public" has functioned for me as a useful prism through which to refract multiple characteristics especially needed in a contemporary theology. My sense is that it brings together several important strands that need to be addressed if theology is to overcome its increasing cultural marginalization. But I have become more sensitive to the dangers of reification that attend reference to something called "public theology." Public theology is a heuristic device that ceases to be useful once questions of inclusion and exclusion drive the discussion.

In retrospect, I have also become more aware of the way in which spotlights create shadows in the very act of illumination. The overriding emphasis on the public realm in this book leaves issues of personal life on the margins. The reconfiguration of public life proposed herein has ramifications for the private realm that remain largely unexplored. I hope my silence is not taken as the measure of their importance.

I am very grateful for the helpful comments and suggestions from colleagues who read the manuscript, in whole or in part: Joel Gereboff, Gordon Kaufman, Richard Martin, Jeffrie Murphy, and Tod Swanson. I would also like to acknowledge the help of the reviewers from SUNY Press for their careful reading of my manuscript. The positive responses gave me incentive to keep working at it, and the criticisms helped me to see much more clearly precisely how. I thank Andrew Christenson for his careful preparation of the index. In addition, I would like to thank Sheila Davaney and Paula Cooey not only for their critical reading of the manuscript but for their friendship and support since our days in graduate school. They have made it far easier and certainly more interesting for me as a theologian.

Chapter 2 and a brief section of chapter 1 were based upon material that originally appeared, respectively in "Hermeneutics and Tradition: The Role of the Past in Jurisprudence and Theology," *Harvard Theological Review* 79, 4 (1986):

439–63 and in "A Model For a Public Theology" *Harvard Theological Review* 80, 2 (1987):193–212, copyright 1986 and 1987 respectively by the president and fellows of Harvard College. Reprinted by permission.

My family and this book have more or less taken shape simultaneously, not always to their mutual benefit. Even though the birth of our two sons, Craig and Jeffrey, may not have contributed to the most timely completion of the manuscript, they have always managed to provide perspective on it and relief from it. But most importantly I want to thank my husband Bob Borengasser, not only for his love and confidence in me, but for his relentless encouragement, ranging from humor to bribes to "babysitting," in completing it.

Chapter One

Religion, Theology, and the Public Realm

Over the past couple of decades a growing number of theologians have begun to insist that religion and theology can and should play a greater role in shaping our public lives. These voices, coming from various quarters, have received considerable attention within the theological community and, in many instances, from the media at large. Consider, for example, the emergence in the 1960s of European political theology in the writings of a Metz or a Moltmann.[1] Commanding even more attention has been the development of Latin American liberation theology with its similar mission to develop a politically effective theology. Within the United States we have witnessed the growth of black and feminist theologies with their respective political and social agendas. On the other side of the political and religious spectrum, we have confronted the meteoric rise of the new Christian right seeking to fashion a "Christian America." These developments clearly cannot be homologized into one movement; they not only reflect incommensurate substantive goals, but they owe their existence to differing local antecedents and contexts. Nevertheless, we can identify a "common enemy" that unites them. Each of these movements is seeking to overcome the privatization of religion. Each is seeking a larger and more effective role for religion and theological discourse in shaping events in the public arena.

This plea for a greater role for religion and theology in shaping our public life has been echoed by others who have been particularly interested in the American scene. Richard John Neuhaus, for example, has argued in his influential book *The Naked Public Square: Religion and Democracy in America* that the American experiment in democracy is

1

seriously threatened by the recent secularization, or, as he would have it, sanitization of our public sphere. Under the ruse that we are a secular, pluralistic society, various forces have succeeded in excluding an appeal to religion or religiously based values in determining our laws and policies. As a consequence, the integrating moral vision he considers necessary both to legitimate and to act as a check upon the law and the power of the state has decayed. The erosion of a shared moral discourse has increasingly left us with the play of power politics and the jockeying of interest groups for shaping our national life. Moral assessment and persuasion have more and more given way to a crude majoritarianism, now considered by many the only way to resolve conflicts in a pluralistic context. Neuhaus contends, however, that the "naked public square" is at most a transitional phenomenon because "transcendence abhors a vacuum."[2] Unless we begin to allow for a larger, more responsible role for the Judeo-Christian traditions in American public life we run the risk, Neuhaus warns, of "an elite construction of a normative morality from sources and principles not democratically recognized by the society."[3] At the moment, he suggests, we are in danger of a totalitarian state or a Christian fundamentalism filling this vacuum.

Robert Bellah has been another vocal critic of the privatization of religion in American life. Although not persuaded that we now confront a naked public square, he shares Neuhaus's sense that biblical religion in America has lost much of its former power to shape our beliefs, values, and sensibilities.[4] This is particularly regrettable, he argues, insofar as the biblical traditions have been largely responsible for cultivating the communal focus that has helped to sustain our liberal democracy. The corrosive effects of modern capitalism combined with the philosophy of secular liberalism have together spawned a rampant individualism that has slowly undermined the moral consensus and communal identity of the American people. Like Neuhaus, Bellah contends that we need to nurture the biblical traditions if we are to dilute the acids of individualism that are corroding the communal mores that undergird our democratic way of life.

While Bellah and Neuhaus focus primarily upon the substantive contributions that biblical religion can make to our public life, others have turned a critical eye upon theology itself. In what respects has theology, following a parallel trajectory, located itself in the private sphere? How has theology conspired, whether knowingly or not, to reinforce its own marginalization? David Tracy argues that some of the blame must indeed be placed upon theologians who have acclimated themselves to the privatization of religion, abandoning all presumptions to speak to or for those outside their narrow communities. Theological arguments have degenerated into dogmatic assertions or confessional accounts of personal beliefs that lack the power or intent to persuade others. As Tracy so aptly puts it, we have fled to local "reservations of the spirit" where we need not confront the wider indifference to and impotence of our work.[5] Seconding this charge, Max Stackhouse insists that what is most urgently needed is a public theology that makes an effort to persuade. He rightly notes that we have plenty of religion in America but very little critical reflection upon it or defense of it. "The land abounds with religious groups, sects, movements, priests, and preachers of all stripes. The problem is that modern religious movements have not made, and seem neither capable of nor interested in making, a case for the truth of what they are talking about in a way that might convince those not already convinced."[6]

The above voices are representative of the recent movement that has begun to speak in terms of a public religion or a public theology. Despite the growing numbers endorsing a more public role and status for religion or theology, there is clearly no consensus on this issue. Indeed many find the conjunction between public and religion or public and theology immediately objectionable. For some it corrupts the character of genuine religion while for others it is not only wrongheaded but a dangerous threat to our pluralistic society.

Public religion to some ears fails to do justice to the intensely personal, private nature of religion. From this angle religion is more a personal religious experience, or as a William James expressed it, "the feelings, acts, and experiences of individual men in their solitude, so far as they apprehend themselves to stand in relation to whatever they may consider the divine."[7] To turn this intensely personal experience into a public phenomenon, then, is to direct attention to secondary external forms not the core experience. However, emphasizing the public character of religion and theology does not require the denial of their connection to the inner, personal dimension. Focusing upon the political or social implications and effects of religious beliefs and practices is more aptly regarded as a corrective to the individualizing trajectory which has tended to assimilate religion to the inner, private world of the autonomous individual.

Those who dismiss the notion of public religion or public theology as wrongheaded, even dangerous, are more numerous. Their fears tend not to stem from a conviction about the essential nature of religion but from a commitment to freedom and pluralism as essential components of the American way of life. There is often a sense, seldom fully articulate, that a public religion or theology in America would transgress the boundary between the separation of church and state. Sometimes operating with a common understanding of public as belonging to the sphere of the government, critics fear that a public religion constitutes an official establishment of religion, a move prohibited by the first amendment to the Constitution. To them a public religion sounds dangerously close to espousing a theocracy in lieu of a democracy. A similar objection is made by those who construe the public not as the state but as the corporate body of "we the people." Insofar as this corporate body displays an array of religious beliefs and affiliations, public religion appears to threaten the religiously plural landscape of American life. Who from the public gets counted in the identification of a public religion? Are Jews or Muslims statistically insignificant when it comes to the articulation of public religion in America? The initial exclusion of religion from the public domain was a hard fought battle to avoid sectarian strife and to ensure freedom of religion for all. Doesn't the effort to reassert the public character of religion threaten to undermine these very real gains?

These are, of course, very serious objections that cannot be lightly dismissed. They make it clear that the terms public religion or public theology cannot be used without substantial clarification. What precisely is meant by public religion? Is it a retrieval of the Durkheimian notion that an integrated society needs a single religious vision? Is there one generic form of public religion or are there many forms of public religion reflecting the multiplicity of religions? How is public religion related to the phenomenon of civil religion, that much discussed and debated concept that Bellah popularized twenty years ago? What are the similarities and differences between public religion and public theology?

The vociferous objections to public religion and public theology can do more than underscore the need for careful distinctions and definitions. They can tip us off as to the nature of the dispute. The relative ease with which calls for a public religion or theology are construed as abridging the constitutional separation of church and state is quite revealing; it suggests that we are dealing here with different ways of interpreting the meaning of public. Advocates of public religion and theology are, whether implicitly or explicitly, objecting to the way in which we have come to configure our public and private spaces. Their proposals amount to a paradigm shift in the public and private geography that we have inherited. It is small wonder that, particularly if this shift goes unrecognized, the notions of public religion or theology strike many as contradictory and dangerous. Therefore, before distinguishing and defining more clearly the nature of public religion and public theology, we need first to attend to the meaning of public. Only by appreciating the variations in this term can we begin to understand the rationale and, perhaps, the legitimation for a public religion and theology.

The Geography of Public and Private

It is easy to assume that the contours of our public and private worlds are permanent features of the social landscape.

The private world encompasses the individual and family, and perhaps intimate friends. The public realm, by definition, would include that world lying beyond our private enclave. What these simple definitions do not capture, however, is the varying ways in which these spheres can be fashioned.[8] In different historical eras human beings have "filled in" these spaces in quite distinctive ways. They have made decisions about such things as the codes of civility, the type of dress, the architectural style, and the forms of discourse that are appropriate in each domain.[9] Just as importantly, the meaning and value of these spheres has varied significantly over the course of history.

The Greek Model

Consider, for instance, the way in which the ancient Greeks construed their public and private worlds.[10] With the rise of the city-states a division between the private life of the family and household and the public sphere of the polis emerged.[11] The family and household were regarded as a natural association belonging to the domain of necessity; this realm catered to the needs of humans to sustain and to reproduce life. The household was a hierarchical domain, with the head of the household wielding primary power. This power was only limited if it conflicted with the interest of the polis. Hence the patriarch, for instance, had complete liberty to sell children or to expose infants to death, for they had no independent rights, protected by the state, proscribing such activities.[12] The polis, on the other hand, was not hierarchically structured. It consisted of a community of equals, each of whom had the right and responsibility to participate in shaping the public life.[13] This egalitarianism had important consequences for determining how the affairs of public life were conducted. Most importantly, it ruled out the use of force or violence on the grounds that such tactics were inappropriate within a community of peers. Debate and persuasion, tactics recognizing and appealing to the heart and mind of the community, were mandated. For the Greeks, participating in this public conversation constituted the life of freedom par excellence. Notice, however, that it was not a freedom *from* all constraints that the Greeks prized most highly. It was the freedom to participate as a citizen in the ongoing conversation of the polis about the appropriate ends of a common life.

The ancient Greeks esteemed the public sphere much more highly than the private. As the domain of freedom, it was the end for which humans were created. "A man who lived only a private life, who like the slave was not permitted to enter the public realm, or like the barbarian had chosen not to establish such a realm, was not fully human."[14] We can see, therefore, that the private sphere was perceived as a privation, as indeed the word indicates; "it meant literally a state of being deprived of something, and even of the highest and most human of man's capacities."[15] The Greeks' attitude toward wealth reflected their relative estimation of the public and private domains. The wealth that an individual accrued in private life was not regarded as an intrinsic good but as that which provided access to the public world, to the realm of freedom. Without wealth an individual was enslaved to procuring the necessities of life and hence was effectively barred from participating in the distinctively human realm of a public conversation amongst equals. Thus while wealth was essential to transcending the sphere of necessity, it was never considered a legitimate end in its own right. "If the property-owner chose to enlarge his property instead of using it up in leading a political life, it was as though he willingly sacrificed his freedom and became voluntarily what the slave was against his own will, a servant of necessity."[16]

The contrast between the Greek vision of the public and private spheres and our own is striking. Whereas the Greeks associated the public world with the exercise of freedom, we are far more likely to consider freedom facilitated in the private sphere. Freed *from* the constraints of the public world, we can give full reign to our feelings and expressions in the refuge of the home. The privative sense of the private sphere has eroded, leaving many with the expectation that the meaning and significance of their lives can be fulfilled within this domain. Nor do we retain the Greek attitude toward the accumulation of wealth. Despite some lingering restraints from a religious ethos, the private accumulation of wealth is no longer considered merely a vehicle enabling one to participate in public life. It has become for many an end in itself. This attitude is, of course, reflected in and reinforced by modern political theory which holds that one of the primary rationales for government is the protection of an individual's right to hold and increase personal wealth.[17] The commonwealth now largely exists for the common *wealth*.[18] The common life of the polis where equals freely participate in debating the meaning of excellence for the body politic has given way to a procedural, watchdog state whose mandate is to secure the private interests of its members.

Lest we romanticize the Greek vision we must point out the underside of their private and public landscape. The public realm was a decidedly restricted sphere. Far from connoting the modern sense of "open to all," the public excluded the vast majority of the populace. Slaves, women, and children were banished to the private domain of necessity; the life of reasoned conversation amongst equals, wherein human identity and excellence were achieved, was only available to a minority. Furthermore, the respective autonomy of the private and public spheres meant that each household had great latitude in conducting its own affairs. Practices that modern society would find reprehensible, and legitimately outlawed, were to the Greeks private affairs. The radical disjunction between the egalitarian public realm and the hierarchical private sphere meant that the power and whims of the paterfamilias, although subject to social disapproval, went otherwise unchecked.

Comparing the Greek and modern ways of configuring and valuing public and private life underscores their historically contingent nature. However, it still leaves us with accounting for the differences. What are the factors that have helped to shape the modern geography of the public and private realm? This, of course, is an enormously complex story that cannot be fully unraveled here. To understand our own interpretation of these realms, however, we must consider, if only briefly, the effect that the Enlightenment has had upon shaping the modern outlook. For this chapter in our history continues to exert its effects long after its official closure.

The Enlightenment Legacy

The Enlightenment influence in the formation of the public and private spheres can be appreciated most fully when set within its own historical context. For the Enlightenment contribution was an intellectual and practical solution to a very real and prolonged crisis in society. It was not some timeless option dreamed up by theorists but the forging of a political and philosophical resolution to pacify a conflict-ridden society. The social crisis that the Enlightenment thinkers faced had its roots in the Protestant Reformation and the lengthy religious wars that ensued in the sixteenth and seventeenth centuries. As scholars have often noted, the Reformation both reflected and greatly exacerbated a crisis of authority within the sixteenth century.[19] Luther's turn to *sola Scriptura* to quell his own uncertainties, and to escape from the cacophony of multiple, conflicting authorities, failed to resolve the problem of authority as the ensuing sixteenth century plainly manifested. The splintering of the reformers into diverse groups, each with its own varied reading of the sacred text, belied the reformers' claims that Scripture was self-interpreting. On the contrary, the multiple readings were ample testimony to the intensification of the crisis of authority not to its resolution. Nor was the Roman Catholic church's response, as reflected in the Council of Trent (1545–63), anything more than a dogmatic reassertion of its own authority. The Protestant Reformation and Catholic Counter-Reformation of the sixteenth century, therefore, constituted a serious impasse over the question of legitimate authority in matters of religious belief and practice. This impasse eventually led to the bloody and disruptive religious wars of the sixteenth and seventeenth centuries.

Against this backdrop of civil and religious discord Enlightenment thinkers sought to demarcate a space that would transcend the sectarian strife. The need was to establish a sphere and an appropriate form of discourse that would avoid the seemingly unresolvable religious controversies that were tearing apart the very fabric of society. The immediate impetus, then, was to develop a secular vocabulary that would be free from divisive religious commitments. To reestablish social peace, religion was increasingly relegated to the sphere of the private, and a secular discourse was developed to articulate the nature of political and social life.

Two of the more important contributors to the creation of this secular discourse were the English Enlightenment theorists Hobbes and Locke; their writings, part of the canon of philosophic liberalism, have had an enormous impact upon the attitudes, behavior, and institutional forms of modern western life. Indeed the assumptions underlying these theories have become so embedded in the personal and political fabric of Western life that they have largely assumed a self-evident quality. It is essential to recognize that these secular theories were not ahistorical or interest-free portraits of human life. They reflected very explicit, historically contingent assumptions about human nature, social life, and the nature of reason.

Basic to philosophic liberalism is the assumption that human beings are radically autonomous creatures who are driven by their desires to pursue their own self-interest. Recognizing the dangers of unrestrained egoism, individuals rationally choose to enter into a social contract that will facilitate their personal security and private gain. Society, according to this view, is not based upon any substantive agreement about the "public good." Indeed, insofar as individuals are naturally disposed to seek their personal interests, there *is* no consensus about the good. Nor need there be, according to liberalism. The most desireable society is one that, as far as possible, maximizes the freedom of individuals to secure their private ends.

The vision of the individual and society at the basis of philosophic liberalism reflected and furthered the social arrangements of the emerging capitalistic economy.[20] Capitalism was breaking the social bonds that had structured the older feudal order; classical liberalism was offering a conception of the autonomous self, unfettered by social relationships, that was eminently suited to the needs of modern capitalism. Not surprisingly, the liberal rationale for pursuing private interest was parallel in the social and economic spheres.

Liberal theory optimistically assumed that the pursuit of private interest would produce the optimal society—one with sufficient order and maximum freedom. Similarly, the underlying assumption of capitalism, reflected in Adam Smith's metaphor of the invisible hand, was that the pursuit of private gain would, through the market economy, produce the optimum public gain. Through this calculus the private interests of individuals and the public welfare were conveniently harmonized.

It is important to recognize the emancipatory thrust of the liberal vision of human life and society. The interwoven strands of its political, social, and economic theory placed primary emphasis upon the autonomy and freedom of the individual. This was a very deliberate intellectual strategy to liberate the social order from the power of entrenched political and ecclesiastical authorities. As William Sullivan notes, "from the seventeenth century to the present the defense of freedom for the individual has been its major theme. The Old Regime in Europe tied political, ecclesiastical, social, and economic institutions together, justifying privilege by appeals to tradition. Thus emancipatory liberalism easily associated escape from injustice with freedom conceived as an end in itself."[21] This emphasis upon the freedom of the individual also spawned a new paradigm of reason that buttressed the political and social implications of the liberal outlook.

To help secure the liberation of the individual and society from the religious and political establishment, Enlightenment thinkers developed a notion of reason that sought to free human thought and practice from the control of heteronomous authorities. Although the Enlightenment paradigm included both rationalist and empiricist variations, its fundamental concern was to free human thought from the chains of tradition. As Kant expressed it in his seminal essay "What Is Enlightenment," reason consists in the capacity to think for oneself, in the refusal to allow outside authorities to determine sound judgment. To the Enlightenment thinkers reason was a distinctively human capacity that we all share. The universal character of reason ensured that inquiry and argument would proceed according to shared criteria, and would, at least potentially, produce a consensus. According to the Enlightenment model, reason is not limited by particularities of time and place. It is an ahistorical capacity that transcends parochial limitations, thereby ensuring that human inquiry need not be dependent upon local authorities or traditions for its assumptions and warrants.

The Enlightenment interpretation of reason took as paradigmatic the style of inquiry that was emerging in the natural sciences of the seventeenth century. It was a style that stressed the requirements of objectivity, neutrality, and a quantitative approach to knowledge. As Sullivan explains, "the new ideal of knowledge was the ability to describe successfully the observable appearances of events in the language of 'simples' and to display their mathematical-logical coherence. . . . Knowledge, then, was knowing things as facts."[22] Insofar as knowledge came to be construed as knowing the facts, it increasingly relegated ideals and goals to a noncognitive status.[23] To know some object was not to know it in light of its telos, but to know it as it appeared. Description and analysis could dispense with the nonempirical concern with ends. A reason modeled upon the empirical sciences might explore what is now the case. It was woefully inadequate, however, to explore what should be the case. However, insofar as ends were considered a matter of private desire, it was to be expected that they fall outside the appropriate provence of reasoned, public inquiry. Ends were a function of the passions, not of reason that might debate their relative merits and reach a consensus. Hence we can see that the trajectory of the Enlightenment interpretation of reason was increasingly to limit reason to the provence of means, denying it a role in the discernment and adjudication of the ends for which we act.[24]

The effects of the liberal interpretations of human nature, society, and reason in shaping our public and private topography in recent centuries have been considerable. To achieve its emancipatory and irenic aims, liberalism, simultaneously, construed "public" in very expansive and very reductive terms. On the one hand, public is highly inclusive insofar as it encompasses all persons. On the other hand, it does not include those aspects of individuals that make them distinct. It "reduces" the individual to a least common denominator of personhood, separating the self from the characteristics and roles that determine personal identity.[25] These specificities that belong to the personal histories of individuals are irrelevant within the public realm. This duality in the meaning of public is also reflected in the Enlightenment model of reason. Reason, in its expansive sense, is a universal capacity shared by all human beings. However, it necessarily excludes the historical determinants or "prejudices" in human reflection that destroy this common character, thereby "reducing" reason to its technical, instrumental function.[26] Hence public has come to have a very inclusive, but very abstract or formal application. Although the most encompassing sphere, it is also the least substantively defined.

The Eclipse of the Public in Contemporary Life

This bivalent meaning of public that the Enlightenment bequeathed is entangled in two dialectically related tendencies that have come to define contemporary life. On the one hand, it has contributed to the expansion of the private sphere in terms of its meaning and significance for human life. "The most revolutionary trait of modern society," Thomas Luckmann has suggested, may be that "personal identity becomes, essentially, a private phenomenon."[27] There clearly can be little interest for the individual in a realm that excludes the specific roles and local affiliations from which we derive our identity. The turn to our private histories and parochial communities as the locus of meaning, therefore, is most apt given the contraction in the meaning of public. The contemporary fascination with psychology, especially analysis, is the logical extension of this trajectory toward locating meaning and purpose within the private realm. As Richard Sennett observes, "Each person's self has become his principal burden; to know oneself has become an end, instead of a means through which one knows the world."[28] To many this trajectory has increasingly felt like a dead end. "Masses of people are concerned with their single life-histories and particular emotions as never before; this concern has proved to be a trap rather than a liberation."[29]

The modern construal of public, however, has also inflamed another movement, dialectically related to this individualizing thrust. Interpreting public in terms of the common, of what we share, has exacerbated the leveling processes at work in modern postindustrial society. The economic, political, social, and technological forces contributing to mass conformism have been well documented. As Josiah Royce, an acute analyst of this phenomenon, has explained:

> because of the spread of popular education, and because of the consolidation and of the centralization of industries and of social authorities, we tend all over the nation, and, in some degree, even throughout the civilized world, to read the same daily news, to share the same general ideas, to submit to the same overmastering social forces, to live in the same external fashions, to discourage individuality, and to approach a dead level of harassed mediocrity.[30]

The leveling processes in modern life are not checked, but sanctioned, when public is defined in terms of commonality. The only escape from such public conformity is the private realm that, perhaps for a time, can protect individuality. This escape, however, is precarious at best. For the trend toward radical individualism and the trend toward an incipient collectivism are not as radically opposed as they might initially appear. They are not conflicting extremes; they are, rather, as John Dewey and Royce, among others, have argued, dialectically related, each intensifying the other in an upward spiral.[31] The retreat to a private realm, therefore, carries with it the ever present danger of a collectivist reversal. The only lasting escape is to break out of the dialectical spiral, to avoid the twin perils of radical individualism and collectivism. Escaping the spiral entails breaking with the entire paradigm of public and private with which it is intertwined.

The ease with which the public, interpreted as the common, slides into mere collectivism, has led some social analysts to speak of the eclipse of the public sphere in the contemporary world. Dewey, for instance, contended that the modernizing forces which destroyed the older local forms of communal life simultaneously eroded a public realm. These modernizing forces have helped produce a "great society," a vast and complex form of life with "lasting, extensive and serious consequences of associated activity."[32] However, there is no organized, conversant public body to explore and debate the far-reaching effects of this vast associational life. For Dewey the public realm is not a collection of individuals who have left their particular histories and commitments at home, but a community of persons who have the desire and resources to debate the relative merits of the various consequences of associational life. The populace, Dewey insisted, lacks both the disposition and the tools to establish this public life. "The essential need," he suggested

> . . . is the improvement of the methods and conditions of debate, discussion and persuasion. That is the problem of the public. We have asserted that this improvement depends essentially upon freeing and perfecting the processes of inquiry and of dissemination of their conclusions.[33]

Hannah Arendt shared Dewey's diagnosis about the eclipse of the public realm, contending that it has been absorbed by society with its mass conformism. She, too, suggested that we have lost sight of a sense of public whose commonality does not eradicate all individual differences. In her words:

> . . . the reality of the public realm relies on the simultaneous presence of innumerable perspectives and aspects in which the common world presents itself and for which no common measurement or denominator can ever be devised. For though the common world is the common meeting ground of all, those who are present have different locations in it, and the location of one can no more coincide with the location of another than the location of two objects. Being seen and being heard by others derive their significance from the fact that everybody sees and hears from a different position.[34]

It sounds somewhat odd to speak of the eclipse of the public sphere when we hear and use the term daily. Indeed it would be less confusing if it were more clearly acknowledged that we are dealing here with different models of public life. Both Dewey and Arendt were attempting to retrieve a notion of public life that has roots within classical Greece.[35] While not embracing the elitism of that model, they were seeking to revive its dialogical and communal dimensions. It is important to recognize that their agenda presupposes a significant transformation in the Enlightenment construal of public. In particular it requires the rejection of the reductive character of the Enlightenment interpretation of public. The public is not a collection of contextless or narrative-free selves—a lowest common denominator of personhood. Nor is the public exercise of reason one that transcends the historical location of these selves. The public is the all-encompassing community of persons who come together to debate and evaluate the effects of their associational life. From this perspective, then, the public is, in an important sense, not fully realized. We currently have too many barriers to the full and equal participation of persons in shaping a communal life. The public, according to this model, must be created through the overcoming of narrow and distorted communication.[36]

This brief excursion into alternate ways of construing the meaning of public illuminates the controversy over calls for a public religion and theology in America. Defenders and critics of public religion and theology, other differences notwithstanding, are talking past one another. Each camp is operating with a different interpretation of public without making sufficiently clear that this is the case. We still stand, in many respects, within the Enlightenment topography of public and private; criticisms of this landscape, as in calls for a public religion and theology, constitute challenges to the long dominant cultural paradigm.[37] The case for a public religion and theology in American life, therefore, coincides with an attack upon our prevailing model for the public realm. Recognizing this connection will prove useful in the next chapter when we consider what it means to engage in a public form of argumentation. The merits of this case, however, cannot be decided in the abstract. We must explore the potential strengths, as well as dangers, of public religion and theology in terms of the specific context to which they are addressed. We have to consider, in other words, the purported ailments affecting contemporary American life that are thought to justify, indeed demand, forms of public religion and theology.

The American Context

Public Virtue and Religion

Calls for a more public face for religion and theology in America coincide with a wider cultural discontent with the state of our national life. There is a growing sense that the liberal capitalistic society of late twentieth century America is seriously flawed. Descriptions of the "cultural crisis" that we face abound, reflected in such works as Daniel Bell's *The Cultural Contradictions of Capitalism* or Christopher Lasch's *The Culture of Narcissism*. Much of the critique is directed against the ethos that has emerged from the confluence of capitalism and philosophic liberalism. It is an ethos that has spawned a radical individualism within American life whose dark underside has grown more and more apparent in recent decades. Liberalism's sanction of the pursuit of personal gain in the social and economic spheres has appeared increasingly shallow, even dangerous, in the light of economic stagnation, growing inequalities in wealth, and depletion of resources. According to many observers, personal success and consumption have become primary ends of American life. Ours has turned into, Roland Delattre argues, a "culture of procurement": the majority of Americans have become "dependent mass consumers with insatiable wants and cravings" whose satisfaction becomes an overriding goal.[38] The liberal expectation that the pursuit of private gain, economically and socially, will produce the optimal society has to many ears taken on a naive, utopian ring whose destructiveness has become progressively more evident in the social pathologies it has spawned.

We have increasingly lost what America's founding figures referred to as "public virtue," the disposition to work towards the improvement of the commonwealth even at significant cost to the self. To a great extent it is the erosion of public virtue within American life that has fueled recent interest in a more public religion. To understand this preoccupation with public religion we must consider, first, why public virtue is considered an indispensable basis for a republic. Secondly, we must explore the historic relationship between public virtue and religion in American life.

Contrary to the *theory* of political and economic liberalism that makes public good a function of private interest, American life has never been solely informed by the liberal outlook. Although moving closer and closer to embodying the liberal ethos, America has also been shaped by the biblical and republican traditions that have historically reflected a much stronger communal emphasis.[39] These more communal traditions have helped to elicit and reinforce a commitment to a common life, thereby tempering the radical individualism of classical liberalism. As Sullivan expresses it, "The ambiguity of America's greatness has always been the coexistence of an economic life of private self-interest with a public commitment to justice and the common welfare."[40] Although our political institutions and economic arrangements reflect the liberal framework, our attitudes and behaviors, at least historically, have been informed by other, less individualistic, motifs. This patchwork combination has, to many minds, been not only a fortuitous but an essential factor in the success and endurance of the American republic. Indeed America's founders recognized that the future of the republic depended upon more than the institutional structures they were erecting; these very structures could only minimize not eradicate the devastating effects of an amoral people. As James Madison noted, "To suppose that any form of government will secure liberty or happiness without any virtue in the people is a chimerical idea."[41] Describing the attitudes of the architects of the American republic, William Lee Miller writes:

...There was wide agreement about the importance of the intellectual and moral condition of the citizenry. These forefathers did want to avoid that cause of the downfall of the republics of the past, a condition they called by terms with an eighteenth-century meaning, "luxury" and "corruption"—the neglect of the public good for private gain, display, advantage, and pleasure: They did want, in their differing ways, to nurture an attachment to the shared human good.[42]

The founders' estimate of the importance of public virtue in sustaining the life of the American republic was echoed fifty years later by Alexis de Tocqueville. If anything de Tocqueville was more adamant about the need for the "habits of the heart" that would temper the privatism and acquisitiveness that he saw growing in nineteenth century America. If left unchecked, he argued, these tendencies posed a serious threat to the fledgling republic. In de Tocqueville's judgment it was largely Christianity, the dominant religion of the American people, that had been responsible for instilling the public virtues needed to sustain a healthy common life. For this reason he insisted that religion in America is "the first of their political institutions."[43] Religion nourishes the communal mores that constitute the essential background for the liberal political and economic framework of American life.

For de Tocqueville, as for contemporary advocates of public religion, Christianity's contribution to the American republic has been crucial insofar as it has been a primary vehicle for the cultivation of the public virtue that is required to sustain a democratic republic. America's founders had already recognized this connection between public virtue and religion in the formation of the cultural mores. In his famous "Farewell Address," George Washington observed that "of all the dispositions and habits which lead to political prosperity, religion and morality are indispensable supports."[44] Although many espoused the Enlightenment notion that morality was in principle separable from religion, they recognized that this was generally the case only for an educated elite. For the vast

majority of the populace, morality was very much a product
of a religious outlook. As Washington, an exponent of this
view, warned:

> And let us with caution indulge the supposition that
> morality can be maintained without religion. What ever
> may be conceded to the influence of refined education on
> minds of peculiar structure, reason and experience both
> forbid us to expect that national morality can prevail in
> exclusion of religious principle.[45]

More recent observers of the American scene have
concurred with Washington's prediction, contending that the
privatization of religion in American life has coincided with
a gradual erosion of moral reflection in public discussions.
In our zealousness to preserve religious freedom, to sustain
a separation between the church and the state, we have
increasingly lost an appropriate vocabulary to examine and
evaluate our public policies and commitments. Writing more
than twenty-five years ago, John Courtney Murray noted a
growing refusal to explore questions of domestic and foreign
policy in light of our moral ideals. Too often we decide such
policy in terms of economic and technical criteria without
raising larger questions about the values and ends guiding
our actions. As Ted Koppel, the popular anchor of "Nightline",
opined, foreign policy is by definition amoral.[46] We have
become habituated to a "cynical divorce between politics and
morality" in discussing the affairs of our common life.[47]

However, despite this ideological exclusion of religion and
morality from public life, in reality the separation is far less
neat. Religious beliefs and moral values do impinge upon
public policy, but their presence is all too often obscured
because of their purported impropriety within public life. We
live out of mythic frameworks with clear religious and moral
dimensions without sufficiently recognizing their power in
shaping our attitudes and behaviors. The sense that America
is a promised land, Americans a chosen people with a mission
to fulfill a divine destiny, for instance, reflects a religious myth
that competes with the "myth of liberalism" in shaping our

identity and practices.[48] However, the moral and religious assumptions underlying this vision generally go unexamined. From this perspective, then, religious and moral perspectives are not so much excluded from public life as their operation and power are obscured because of the prevailing ideology that has purportedly relegated them to the private realm.

Public Religion, Civil Religion, and Public Theology

Public religion, so its defenders suggest, has the potential to redress some of the failings associated with our public life. However, it is not every form of religiosity that can fill this role; indeed many forms of religion in American society merely exacerbate the problems of our public life. Numerous scholars have noted that American religion has increasingly lost its ability to elicit the public virtues that the founding fathers considered indispensable to the life of the republic. Many of the strands within American Christianity have tended to absorb rather than to temper the individualizing tendencies of the wider culture.[49] Hence if Christianity is to retrieve its earlier power to fashion a public virtue, it will require reformulation, a renewed emphasis upon the communal dimensions and responsibilities of human life. Calls for a public religion, therefore, are not aimed at giving any and every religion a public voice. They are, rather, pleas for the self-transformation of religion, for the "theological retreading" of religion so that it may again contribute to the sustenance and critique of the common weal.

It is important to differentiate this interpretation of public religion from the phenomenon of "civil religion" that has elicited much study and debate within the past two decades. Although closely related in the problematic being addressed, they are not equivalent. Robert Bellah appropriated the concept of civil religion to refer to that core of religious symbols and assumptions that have informed the dominant self-understanding of the American people throughout its history. This religious self-understanding has been "institutionalized" in important texts of our founding fathers, presidents, and Supreme Courts. Consider, for instance, the references in the Declaration of Independence to the sovereignty of God, or the religious symbolism in Washington's Farewell Address and Lincoln's Gettysburg Address. Although such religious references have no legal standing, they have reflected and reinforced a common religious vision that has played a significant role in shaping our national self-understanding. These minimal references to the sovereignty of the Creator God sprinkled throughout prominent political addresses in American history have been supplemented by the personal faith of the American people. The Protestant alliance that came to cultural domination in the nineteenth century combined with the minimal biblical religiosity institutionalized in political texts to produce a powerful and deeply rooted religious self-understanding. "To be an American was to be part of a pilgrim people in covenant with a transcendent power, a people who had been given a promised land and a manifest destiny."[50] Although this religious vision may indeed have provided Americans with a common self-understanding, a common identity, it is important to note that this shared civil religion has been dependent upon the dominance of Protestant Christianity within the culture at large. In other words, the existence of an American civil religion has been a product of the symbiosis of the formal, minimal religiosity institutionalized in political discourse, and the more pluriform and concrete creedal beliefs and symbols of the Protestant denominations.

The ambiguities in the concept of "civil religion" have led some, including Bellah, to abandon its usage. Speaking of a common civil religion in America obscures the role that the specific denominational groups have played in sustaining this shared vision. This is particularly worrisome as we witness the decline of Protestantism's hegemony in American culture. Forcefully making this point, John F. Wilson writes:

> Where there is a common religion, a civil religious tradition is essentially a specification—perhaps institutionalization— of its values, symbols, and myths, and may prove to be an effective means of making broadly based cultural values influential within the political arena. Absent a common religion, however, and a civil religion becomes a scarcely

veiled revitalization movement, perhaps intensely reactionary in its program, dedicated to returning a culture to the value complex believed to have dominated a previous time. Far from representing a movement that may be constructive in relationship to the whole society, civil religion in the absence of the common religion as background seems necessarily to be highly selective, prejudicial, indeed, one among other religious movements contending for control of the society in question.[51]

Public religion, in contrast to civil religion, does not necessarily mean a shared set of religious symbols and beliefs that inform a society, thereby conferring a common identity and self-understanding upon a people. Rather than requiring a common religious vision, public religion refers to the way in which a specific religious tradition or community appropriates its distinctive resources to contribute to the upbuilding of the common life. As Martin Marty has argued, the concept of public religion is more suited to America's pluralistic landscape than is civil religion which presumes a social and religious uniformity within a people:

> This term from Benjamin Franklin fits the American pluralist pattern better than does Rousseau's civil religion because it took account of the particularities of the faiths that would not disappear or lightly merge to please other founders of the nation. These churches could, however, contribute out of their separate resources to public virtue and the common weal.[52]

Civil religion highlights a watered-down, minimalist religiosity which, presumably, is largely shared by the populace. By necessity it focuses on "generic" religion. Public religion, on the other hand, while not excluding the possibility of a civil religion, is a function of "brand-name" religion. Rather than identifying a common religious vision uniting a people, public religion attends to the way in which particular religious traditions cultivate and nurture a common life within the society at large. For this reason public religion will include many exemplifications, reflecting the diversity of concrete religions as they order and valorize public life.

But the notion of public religion, like that of civil religion, obscures the role and importance of theological reflection upon religion. The distinctive character and problems of developing a public theology are overlooked when it is absorbed into the concept of public or civil religion. There clearly is a close connection between religion and theology as they have developed in Western religious traditions, especially Christianity. We often speak, for instance, of a Christian worldview as a theological vision, more or less equating the ideational and symbolic dimensions of religion with theology. Furthermore, during much of its legacy Christian theology has been considered a religious exercise, intellectual activity in the service of faith, making it difficult to draw any clear distinction between theology and religious faith. However, the significant differences between religion and theology have become more apparent, indeed more pronounced, in our own time. While it is important to maintain the connection between religion and theology, it is also essential to recognize their distinction, particularly in the effort to develop a more public theology. The distinction between religion and theology must be carefully maintained to preserve the critical and constructive dimensions of theology. For centuries theology was largely considered the interpretation of Scripture and dogma which had been divinely revealed to humans. Hence theology might render religious beliefs more understandable but it was not fully recognized as a source for the creation or reconstruction of beliefs and dogmas. Edward Farley's historical account of classical Christian theology explains the practice and assumptions of this traditional form of reflection:

> The criteria, evidences, and givens for theological work reside in dogmas or doctrinalizations. . . .The intellectual work which attends the church's teaching office is primarily setting forth, understanding, and clarifying the doctrinal given. When new questions and issues do occur, the way they are settled is by citation of the authority: a scriptural text, a Church Father, Church Council, or papal declaration. The theologian's relation to the authority is hermen-

eutical in character. The agenda which the authority sets is to interpret and apply, not assess.[53]

It has become apparent to many, however, that this traditional understanding of theology is seriously deficient. It fails to account adequately for the critical and constructive role of the theologian in the passing on of a tradition.

The dialectical relationship between religion and theology ensures overlap and affinity between a public religion and a public theology. Although the goal of a public theology, I will argue, includes the facilitation of public religion, this substantive agenda is not an exhaustive criterion. Because theology is a reflective practice, involving the critical reflection upon and transformation of religion, it demands attention in its own right. The defining characteristics of public theology will not be reducible to those of public religion, then, however much their substantive intentions may overlap.

A Model for a Public Theology

Our discussion thus far provides a preliminary indication of the nature of a public theology. Perhaps most basically, a public theology seeks to overcome the cultural marginalization so highly characteristic of contemporary theology. It seeks, furthermore, to contribute to the upbuilding and critical transformation of our public life. It refuses to remain confined to a private sphere, dealing with issues of personal spirituality, salvation, and ethics. This definition, however, remains far too general. It fails to specify *how* a public theology carries out this self-appointed task. Is any theology that deals with large social and political issues to be considered a public theology? Are the theologies of the new Christian evangelical right genuinely public? Are the Latin American liberation theologies appropriate models of a public theology? I think not. Although both of these types seek to overcome the privatization and marginalization of theological reflection, their methods of argumentation are, for the most part, not public. They generally remain confessional theologies, appealing to theological authorities to defend their positions. Hence, a public theology is not merely a synonym for a political theology, despite the important similarities between them. A public theology not only must address itself to the wider social and political issues, but it must appropriate a form of argumentation that is genuinely public.

Given the historicity of all reflection, no discourse should expect or hope to be universally intelligible let alone persuasive. Public theology, eschewing the impossible ideal of universal intelligibility, will situate itself within a recognizable tradition and communicate primarily, although not exclusively, to inhabitants of that tradition. For a public theology, however, this inevitable situatedness does not legitimate confessional or authoritarian modes of reflection. Because of the importance of engaging in a public mode of argumentation, the moral and religious warrants for which will be considered in subsequent chapters, we cannot define public theology solely in terms of its substantive agenda. It is not merely breaking out of the arena of privatism that constitutes a public theology. Indeed it is not any single criterion that defines a public theology, but several in combination. If theology is to expand its audience and influence, it will need to attend to the variety of its features that undermine a public character.

There are a number of reasons for theology's failure to enjoy a public impact and status. These reasons, of course, vary across constituencies. Some, particularly those within the academy, have dismissed theology as a parochial form of apologetics in which assertion parades as argument. Others, concerned more with practice than with theory, consider its content irrelevant, unable to illuminate the difficult choices facing us. And many others, finally, simply find it unintelligible. If we are to find labels for these reasons, we might say that theology's exclusion from the public realm is due to its perceived parochialism, privatization, and professionalization. That is, many consider it to display a parochial confessionalism, a preoccupation with issues of private spirituality, and a highly professionalized style. Despite recent, auspicious signs of change, much twentieth century theology has been marked by these features, accounting, to a great extent, for its exclusion from the public sphere.

The sociological, historical, and philosophical developments that have contributed to the marginalization of
theological reflection are not easily reversed. Indeed many
of the factors lie beyond the control of those in the field.
Nonetheless, some constructive steps are possible to minimize
theology's current plight. For theologians have, whether
wittingly or not, become accomplices in the exclusion of
theology from public discourse.

The following chapters seek to develop a model for a public
theology that takes account of the multiple factors responsible
for the exclusion of theology from the public conversation.
The second chapter will explore what it means to engage in
a public form of argumentation. What are the methodological
assumptions and procedures of a reflective practice that
aspires to a public status? To identify such assumptions and
procedures we will need to consider the nature of reason and
its relationship to historical context, tradition, and authority.
I shall argue that we need to break out of the Enlightenment
framework that has interpreted reason and public in terms
of what is common, objective, and unaffected by historical and
social location. Nevertheless, we must retain the Enlightenment insight into the difference between citation and inquiry
by continuing to reject argument from authority. This will
enable us to identify a form of theological argumentation that
locates itself within a recognizable tradition of interpretation,
but which eschews the authoritarian or confessional tendencies of much theology.

After identifying the methodological features that mark
a public form of argumentation, we will turn in chapter 3
to a consideration of the substantive aim of a public theology.
What role can theology play within the public realm? In order
to address this question it is necessary to explore more fully
than we have the prevailing interpretation of public life in
America. This chapter, then, will focus upon the public/private
topography that has come to dominate a wide segment of
American culture, and identify the intellectual and social
forces that have created it. I will argue that a critical role
for theology in American public life is the exposure and
critique of the assumptions and effects of the prevailing

public/private paradigm. Public theology must work toward the reconfiguration of this paradigm. The most pressing need is to cultivate a sense of public life as not simply a collectivity of individuals with private ends but a genuine common life within which individuals share significant goals. Such a revisioning of public life tempers the radical individualism of the reigning model by highlighting the myriad interconnections that bind individuals in a complex reciprocating field. This reconfiguration of the public realm points the way toward a global identity that is formed in and through more local communities rather than in opposition to them. Public life, from this perspective, is not an abstract vessel containing separate units but the inclusive fabric of interconnections binding individuals into a common life.

Following these historical and philosophical explorations of the public realm, chapter 4 adopts a more explicitly theological perspective. This chapter seeks to demonstrate the way in which commitment to God, properly interpreted, generates powerful legitimation for the proposed reconfiguration of public life. From this analysis it becomes clear that the task of a public theology is not mandated by external, pragmatic reasons alone but reflects an agenda that is deeply rooted within the tradition of Christianity itself.

If theology is to gain a greater voice in shaping the public realm, however, it is impossible to ignore the complex of issues connected with the style of contemporary theological writing. Chapter 5 argues that the "professionalization" of American life in the twentieth century has contributed to the formation of theology as an intellectual genre that has little impact or intelligibility beyond a small circumscribed professional guild. Although these professionalizing forces within theology have historical antecedents, their presence has become especially troubling when combined with other factors contributing to the marginalization of theology in contemporary culture. The development of a public theology, therefore, is inextricably connected to resisting the excessive professionalization of the genre as a whole.

The final chapter, drawing together some of the threads from the preceding chapters, offers a final overview of the proposed reconfiguration of the public realm and the form of theology most conducive to its emergence. In this chapter I seek to address some of the problems and perhaps offset some misperceptions that might arise from the following portrait of public life and theology.

Chapter Two

Theology and Public Argumentation

Public religion and public theology, as noted earlier, are not the same thing even though the intimate relationship between religion and theology ensures their overlap. If public theology could be identified exclusively in terms of its role in enhancing the impact of religion in public life, it would be indistinguishable from public religion. There would be no expectations concerning how a religion should wield this power and influence. All tactics would be legitimate, including indoctrination and coercion. Theology, however, is a reflective practice not simply a substantive belief; the methodological assumptions and procedures of this practice can be specified. A public theology, therefore, denotes more than the substantive agenda that it shares with public religion. Just as importantly, it signifies the embrace of a public form of argumentation.

It is this requirement that most people would consider the insurmountable obstacle to the creation of a public theology. How can theology be construed as a public form of inquiry? Within most circles, whether in the academy or the culture at large, theology is regarded as a parochial exercise. Rather than appealing to a common human experience, theology typically roots itself in the experiences and texts of a specific religious community. Instead of employing discourse that all share, theology appropriates the symbols and motifs of a particular tradition. Rather than engage in open inquiry, theology appears to take as axiomatic certain "truths" as the givens of its reflection. Theology is parochial in the sense that it not only addresses a particular religious community but it appeals to the symbols, experiences, and texts of that community for its justification. This rootedness in a particular religious tradition is thought to preclude the public nature of theological argumentation. Indeed, from this perspective, theology is more aptly construed as a product of faith, not reason, as a confessional exercise that does not embody genuine argumentation at all. Far from undertaking objective, open inquiry, theology resorts to citation through its appeal to religious authorities. For this reason, many have argued that theology does not properly belong within the university with its commitment to open inquiry. As parochial discourse it belongs within the enclave of the churches that presumably share its unquestioned assumptions and authorities. The Vatican's challenges to Hans Kung or Charles Curran reflect and reinforce this view of theology within academia and the wider society. What academic integrity can a discipline have when acceptable boundaries are determined not by its practitioners but by external authorities?

This view about the parochial nature of theology is not limited to critics outside the field. Theologians themselves have sometimes voiced a similar position insofar as they conceive of theology as a confessional activity. Accepting the basic tenets and texts of their tradition as authoritative, they understand themselves to be essentially engaged in a translation process, restating the fundamentals of the tradition in a contemporary idiom.

If the above depiction of the parochial character of theology were fully adequate, then we would have no choice but to abandon the quest for a public form of theological argumentation. This depiction, however, collapses two different ways of understanding the parochial nature of theology. It is important to distinguish between them because they are not equally damning. The first sense of parochial refers to theology's appropriation of and engagement with the texts, symbols, and experiences of a particular tradition. The second sense captures theology's dependence upon certain first principles or authorities that have traditionally circumscribed theological argumentation. We must differentiate between these two senses of parochial because they constitute different obstacles for developing a public theology.

To assume that theology is not a form of public discourse because of its engagement with a particular tradition presumes a highly misleading ahistorical sense of public; rather than acquiesce to this ahistorical notion of public, theologians should help to combat the prejudice against tradition that it reflects. This ahistorical interpretation of the meaning of public and the public exercise of reason reflects, as we have seen, the Enlightenment legacy that continues to inform our outlook. Developing a public theology, therefore, depends upon breaking free from the Enlightenment construal of public with its impossible ideal of nontraditioned inquiry and argumentation.

It does not mean, however, completely rejecting the Enlightenment ideal. Although subject to distortion, the Enlightenment distinction between engaging in open inquiry and citing heteronomous authorities reflected an important insight that must be retained. There is some danger, I think, that "postmodernism" and its defense of the traditioned character of all reflection will be appropriated by theologians to legitimate confessional, authoritarian forms of theology.[1] The problem, then, lies in differentiating between an illegitimate, authoritarian parochialism and a legitimate parochialism, more aptly called contextualism. The aim of this chapter is to clarify and defend this distinction. If successful, it makes room for a form of theology that self-consciously operates out of an identifiable tradition without thereby abandoning the commitment to open inquiry: in other words, a public theology, reflecting a suitably chastened, historicist construal of public.

Tracy and the Publicness of Theology

We can begin to gain some clarification about what it means to engage in a public form of argumentation by considering David Tracy's exploration of this issue. He, as much as any theologian, has been particularly concerned to demonstrate that theology must indeed be considered a public form of discourse. By virtue of theology's preoccupation with

God, understood as that necessarily universal reality, theologians must not rest content with private confessions of faith that seek neither to inform nor persuade others.[2] For Tracy, however, the way in which a theologian strives for publicness will vary according to the particular audience he or she is addressing. Insofar as the public is not one homogeneous whole but composed of various social realities with distinct traditions, values, and assumptions, the theologian must tailor a theology to the primary public for which it is written.

Consider, for instance, the two forms of public theology that Tracy develops, respectively, for the academy and for the church: fundamental theology and systematic theology.[3] Although acknowledging that each type appropriates a different sense of "public," Tracy argues that each, nevertheless, constitutes a legitimate form of public address suitable to the assumptions of a specific audience. Fundamental theology deals with issues of religious meaning and truth that are potentially intelligible to all reasoning persons. It presupposes, Tracy contends, "the first and obvious meaning of publicness (viz., as meaning and truth available to all intelligent, reasonable and rational persons through persuasive argument). . . ."[4] Systematic theology, on the other hand, initially appears to be decidedly nonpublic insofar as it appropriates symbols, doctrines, and texts that are rooted in specific traditions. Such particularity, however, need not preclude publicness. Closely following Hans-Georg Gadamer, Tracy argues that classics in both art and religion achieve a genuine publicness "because of, not in spite of, an intensified particularity."[5] Thus he writes, "although radically particular in origin and expression, the classics are public in our second sense: grounded in some realized experience of a claim to attention, unfolding as cognitively disclosive of both meaning and truth and ethically transformative of personal, social and historical life."[6]

The two different senses of public underlying fundamental and systematic theology warrant markedly different theological tasks. Fundamental theology, appealing to common human religious experiences, explores metaphysical questions and necessarily remains at an abstract level. Systematic theology entails the interpretation of the religious classics of a tradition, thereby enabling a more concrete form of reflection. Tracy is careful to allow each subdiscipline substantial independence, being particularly apprehensive that fundamental theology be regarded as a substitute for or external judge of conversation with the religious classics. Far from usurping the role of systematic theology, fundamental theology can buttress its importance by demonstrating the existence of the religious dimension in human experience, thereby legitimating the engagement with a particular religious tradition.

Tracy has made a considerable contribution to theology in calling attention to the importance of reaffirming its public character. However, his defense of the publicness of these forms of theology rests upon an equivocation in the meaning of "public." Far from being analogous meanings of one term, his two senses of public, presupposing different understandings of the nature of reason, are not readily assimilable. Indeed they reflect markedly different orientations and assumptions, suggesting that they belong to incommensurate paradigms.

Fundamental theology engages in reasoned argument, dealing with questions and answers "which any attentive, intelligent, reasonable and responsible person can understand and judge in keeping with fully public criteria for argument."[7] This interpretation of public reflects the Enlightenment model of reason, understood as a universal, ahistorical capacity of all rational beings. Much modern philosophy, however, including figures such as Nietzsche, Wittgenstein, Heidegger, and Gadamer, has sought to combat the hold that this Enlightenment picture of reason has exerted over Western consciousness.[8] Discounting the myth of an ahistorical, universally shared human reason, philosophers have increasingly stressed that reason is inextricably rooted in a specific historical and cultural matrix. Reflection takes place in and through a linguistic medium that reflects the assumptions, values, and interests of a particular place and time. A common human reason or common human experience is, from this historicist perspective, a false construct that obscures the irreducible particularity of human life and reflection. Indeed Tracy himself accepts this critique when he insists on the need to acknowledge a second "less obvious" sense of public, one which recognizes that reason is inextricably informed by the particular symbols, texts, and events of a tradition. If this second sense of public reflecting a contextual interpretation of reason is granted, it undermines rather than supplements the more common understanding. In other words, the two interpretations of public with their correlative notions of reason are incommensurable, belonging to markedly different horizons. To grant the historical location of human reflection is to abandon the Enlightenment ideal of objectivity, the transcendence of particularity.

This has significant implications for the development of a public theology. First, it suggests that Tracy's fundamental theology and systematic theology can only be simultaneous candidates for public theology through a vacillation in the meaning of public. The fact that these types of theology are addressed to significantly different audiences does not justify the vacillation. Furthermore, the strong case that has been constructed against the Enlightenment pretensions to universality and objectivity seriously undermines the notions of public and rationality underlying fundamental theology.

His interpretation of systematic theology, in my judgment, offers far more promise for the development of a public theology. His defense of this form of theology rests upon an understanding of public that recognizes the effects of concrete traditions in the exercise of human reflection. Hence in the process of proposing systematic theology as a candidate for public theology, Tracy points toward the reconstrual of public that this necessarily entails. This is critical to the effort to articulate a public form of theology.

The model of public theological argumentation that I shall defend in this chapter follows the direction of Tracy's systematic theology in important respects. But it seeks to emphasize and clarify more fully the constructive side of theology. The hermeneutical model of theology that Tracy defends appears to constrain theologians to the interpretation of the classics.[9] While Tracy clearly allows for, indeed encourages, a hermeneutics of suspicion in the interpretive process, this hermeneutical model does not adequately account for the constructive, creative dimension of theology.[10] I will come back to this point later in the chapter as I attempt to sketch out a more adequate model for a public theology. First, however, it is necessary to consider more fully the very important insights into the historicity and particularity of human reflection that inform Tracy's vision of public theology.

Reason and Tradition

We have to look more closely at the claim that reason is always shaped by its historical and social location. For it is only by way of this affirmation that we can recognize that theological reflection rooted in a specific religious tradition does not necessarily forswear its public character. Affirming the contextual nature of reflection entails a fundamental rejection of the Enlightenment understanding of reason; indeed it constitutes the primary sign of what has increasingly been called the transition to postmodernity. To escape from the heteronomous domination of reason, the Enlightenment interpreted reason as a universal capacity of each human being. The responsible exercise of this capacity was modeled upon the sciences; judgments should be based upon empirical evidence and, potentially, be confirmable by all reasoning persons. Spheres of inquiry that failed to meet this test of objectivity lost status, gradually being relegated to the realm of subjectivity, inaccessible to reasoned, public debate. Despite its continued hold over the popular imagination, the Enlightenment ideal of objectivity has been increasingly attacked for failing to account for the historical determinants in all knowledge. All forms of inquiry, including science, are dependent upon intellectual traditions that determine the warrants as well as the questions that are recognized.[11] The Enlightenment goal of eliminating all forms of prejudice from reason was, as Gadamer has argued, itself a prejudice which has led to the popular construal of reason as instrumental and of values as subjective.[12]

Many thinkers and movements in contemporary philosophy, as noted earlier, have sought to underscore this historicist interpretation of human reflection. Gadamer, one of the more articulate and accessible spokespersons for this position, directly challenges the modern pretensions to objectivity in the development of his hermeneutical philosophy. Rejecting the model of objectivity that posits a neutral, ahistorical appropriation of the other, Gadamer attempts to show that all understanding is necessarily perspectival, an interpretation of the other that is influenced by the assumptions, needs, and interests of the interpreter. The Enlightenment model of objectivity, rooted in its quest for autonomous reason, fails to acknowledge the historicity of the knowing subject that inevitably colors all interpretation of the other.

Emphasizing the perspectival character of all interpretation is not a form of solipsism, a denial that we can indeed know the other, but a necessary corrective to the objectivist fallacy that gripped the Enlightenment and its contemporary progeny. Developing Heidegger's model of the hermeneutical circle, Gadamer argues that all understanding takes place in and through dialogue. The interpreter approaches a text with a certain preunderstanding and through a to-and-fro engagement with the subject matter attempts to develop an appropriate interpretation. The influence of one's own horizon which makes understanding a process of interpretation prompts Gadamer to claim that "we understand in a different way, if we understand at all."[13] Understanding is a "fusion of horizons" that is not merely a re-production of the other but a new historical appropriation of the other, a new perspective on the other.

To recognize the historical character of the reasoning process is to recognize that humans do not reflect in isolation from their traditions but in and through them. From this perspective, it is simply false to claim that moral philosophy, for instance, engages in public inquiry whereas religious ethics necessarily does not. The traditions informing moral philosophy tend to be less visible than those informing religious ethics.[14] The "parochial" character of an ethic that finds the life of Jesus morally compelling leaps out at us whereas an appeal to a Kantian respect for persons does not. The reasons for this are, again, rooted in the Enlightenment project. To overcome the sectarian strife of the sixteenth century, theorists developed a secular discourse that preempted the public square. The historically contingent, interest-laden character of the values and ideals informing this discourse were obscured. Hence, we have largely bought into the opposition between secular, public discourse and religious, parochial discourse. Certain interests continue to be served through the perpetuation of this particular opposition. As Neuhaus rightly notes

> . . . intellectuals have a monopoly on the interpretation of classical belief systems. The exegesis of Aristotle and Plato is reserved to the academy, whereas the exegesis of the Bible is a mass industry employing millions of professional and part-time believers. Choosing classical religion over biblical religion protects public philosophy as an aristocratic enterprise. It does not threaten the monopoly of the certified keepers and definers of the sacred cultural symbols.[15]

Underscoring the contextual nature of all reflection, however, does not fully deflect the charge that religious reflection is parochial. After all, insiders and outsiders alike have noted that religious folks as well as theologians often speak and argue as if their sources were privileged in a manner not available, in principle, to other sources. This tendency is not addressed in the above portrait of the traditioned form of all human inquiry. But it is essential to account for this tendency, and this for two reasons, one more salient to critics of theology and the other to some of its practitioners. First, if left unaddressed, one of the primary factors leading to the charge that theology is parochial is simply ignored, making a move from the contextual nature of all reflection to the conclusion that theology is public much too hasty and unconvincing. Secondly, this ascription of parochial to theology is sometimes justified, making it imperative that theologians who aspire to a form of public theology recognize the distinction, to be explored further below, between contextual and parochial reflection.

To reiterate, theology's rootedness within a particular tradition does not automatically brand it as a form of parochial discourse. It is necessary to determine *how* a theology makes use of the texts, symbols, and creeds of a tradition. There is a significant difference between a theology that takes these constitutive elements of its tradition as resources and one that grants special privilege to one or more of these elements as isolated authorities.[16] The latter subverts the ideal of open inquiry that modernity has rightly embraced as a defining characteristic of public discourse.

Theology and Jurisprudence

In order to gain greater clarity about the way in which theology engages the tradition within which it is embedded I propose to consider the relationship between theology and jurisprudence. I am following through on a suggestion Gadamer makes concerning the paradigmatic nature of legal hermeneutics, particularly judicial argumentation, for understanding the interpretive process.

We have already noted Gadamer's contention that understanding is necessarily perspectival, a process of interpretation that entails a to-and-fro engagement between the horizon of the interpreter and the subject matter being addressed. Just as understanding and interpretation cannot be separated into sequential moments, Gadamer insists that application is not a secondary practical concern but an intrinsic component of the one hermeneutic act of understanding/interpretation/application.[17] The interpretation of the other always presupposes the horizon of the interpreter, a situation out of which and for which an interpretation occurs. Gadamer notes that the centrality of application in hermeneutical understanding was eclipsed in the eighteenth and nineteenth centuries as historical and literary studies set themselves up as the hermeneutical paradigm; an emphasis upon disclosing the other in its historical and cultural horizon obscured the recognition of the determinative influence of the interpreter's interests, questions, and assumptions. To rectify this misleading view of the hermeneutical process, Gadamer proposes that we consider legal interpretation the most appropriate paradigm for hermeneutical understanding. In making a legal decision, the judge is attempting to interpret the law not in abstraction, but as it applies to a specific concrete case. By emphasizing that interpretation is shaped by situational interests and needs, this model is a better illustration of the hermeneutical unity of understanding/interpretation/application. Thus Gadamer writes that "legal hermeneutics is able to point out what the real procedure of the human sciences is. Here we have the model for the relationship between past and present that we are seeking."[18]

I want to pursue Gadamer's contention that legal hermeneutics, particularly jurisprudence, constitutes the paradigmatic form of interpretation. Considering various ways the past constrains judicial decisions illuminates the role of the past in theological reflection. Although the differing aims and roles of the theologian and the judge rule out any exact analogy between law and theology, there are sufficient similarities to warrant the comparison. More specifically, an exploration of the methodological appropriations of the past in jurisprudence illuminates and lends support to the proposed distinction between contextualism and parochialism. In addition, it sheds light on the theologian's concern to interpret and extend a particular tradition, an interest that distinguishes it from many other forms of inquiry.

Dworkin's Typology of Judicial Argumentation

I shall explore the various ways in which the past constrains judges in making their decisions by considering a typology of judicial reasoning that Ronald Dworkin, a philosopher of law, has developed.[19] He distinguishes three primary forms of judicial interpretation that reflect different methodological assumptions and tactics: conventionalism, naturalism, which I shall call extensionalism, and instrumentalism.[20] These forms of judicial reasoning differ primarily in regard to the way the past informs and constrains the judge's decisions. Without becoming embroiled in all the complexities and nuances of Dworkin's typology, I shall briefly sketch out the defining characteristics of each type, and then consider their relationship to forms of theological argumentation.

Conventionalism is the name given to that type of judicial adjudication in which decisions are made on the basis of precedents.[21] According to this theory, the proper task of the judge is first to identify the persons or institutions that have been authorized to make law within a given society. The judge proceeds to investigate whether such lawful authorities have established a rule that unambiguously applies in the current case. If there is such a rule, then the judge is bound to follow it. If there is no such rule, the judge may make a new ruling which becomes part of the body of authoritative precedents that guides later decisions. The judge, therefore, has the leeway to make novel decisions, reflecting his or her own political and moral proclivities, only when the past does not set a precedent for how such cases are to be decided.

Underlying this approach is the assumption that appropriate legal precedents can be identified in a fairly straightforward manner. As Dworkin carefully demonstrates, however, it is far from apparent that, with the exception of the easiest cases, judges can isolate the relevant legal precedents and elucidate their meaning without an elaborate process of interpretation that inevitably involves moral and political considerations. The very meaning of the law is not mechanically apprehended but is interpreted, an activity that is inseparable from moral and political judgments.[22]

Arguing this point, Dworkin observes that legal disagreements arise

> not only about what the Constitution and laws of our nation should be but also about what they are. . . . Interpretation of the Equal Protection Clause of the United States Constitution provides especially vivid examples. There can be no useful interpretation of what that clause means which is independent of some theory about what political equality is and how far equality is required by justice, and

the history of the last half-century of constitutional law is largely an exploration of exactly these issues of political morality. Conservative lawyers argued steadily (though not consistently) in favor of an author's intentions style of interpreting this clause, and they accused others, who used a different style with more egalitarian results, of inventing rather than interpreting law. But this was bluster meant to hide the role their own political convictions played in their choice of interpretive style, and the great legal debates over the Equal Protection Clause would have been more illuminating if it had been more widely recognized that reliance on political theory is not a corruption of interpretation but part of what interpretation means.[23]

The assumption that judges can follow relevant precedents without being swayed by personal dispositions, both moral and political, is not supported, Dworkin argues, by historical study. Thus, by restricting the judge's creative input to cases that lack relevant legal precedents, conventionalism appears to be advocating a methodological policy that is simply impossible to carry through.

Dworkin criticizes conventionalism, however, not simply for making the past too determinative in judicial decisions but for making it too irrelevant. When a judge fails to find a relevant precedent to follow, conventionalism assumes that judges should invent new law. Thus in the absence of an exact precedent, the past becomes irrelevant to the judge's decision.

Extensionalism, Dworkin's second form of judicial interpretation, differs from conventionalism by making the past less constraining in one sense and more constraining in another. Rather than identify isolated rules or laws that it must strictly follow, extensionalism seeks to interpret the laws and their underlying principles viewed as a whole and in their best light.[24] Although this approach makes any single isolated precedent less constraining, it grants the past, broadly interpreted, a more significant role in the interpretive process. In order to clarify the type of judicial interpretation that extensionalism embodies Dworkin develops a very illuminating illustration involving a chain novel.[25] Suppose a novel were being written through the efforts of many authors working serially rather than in collaboration. You received the first three chapters of the novel and had been asked to write the fourth chapter. In order to help create a good novel, it would be necessary to pay careful attention to the plot and to the established characterizations, among other things. An incoherent plot or arbitrarily depicted set of characters would hardly constitute a good novel. Even given the constraints of the first three chapters you would, nevertheless, be obliged to create new plot twists, and deeper and more extensive character observations if you were to write the next chapter. Suppose you wanted to continue the story in a direction that allowed you to articulate an important insight about the human condition. The first three chapters did not contradict this motif but neither did they directly suggest it. Even though this theme did not "fit" as well with the first three chapters as other possible themes, you might decide its urgency justified continuing the novel in order to accommodate it. In short, when deciding how to continue the novel, your choice would depend upon how well it "fit" with the preceding chapters as a whole and upon how well it articulated substantial insights, from your own lights, about human experience.

Continuing a chain novel is analogous to making judicial decisions according to the framework of extensionalism. The judge will be concerned that his or her decision fits past rulings. However, those past rulings are not interpreted in isolation but in the widest possible context, the context that makes the best sense of law and the political order as a whole. It is this latter stricture that differentiates this form of adjudication from the conventionalist type. As the following example discloses, this methodological variance can yield significantly different concrete decisions.

> Suppose a firm line of cases has rejected the idea that clients may sue lawyers who are negligent. Conventionalism is then committed (so it might be said) to continuing that doctrine until it is reversed by legislation, which seems the democratic solution. But [extensionalism] encourages judges to put this line of cases in a wider context, and ask

whether the rule refusing recovery against negligent lawyers would not itself be rejected by the best justification of the rest of the law, which allows recovery for negligent injury of almost every other kind. So [an extensionalist] might be led to overrule these cases, which a conventionalist would leave for the legislature to review.[26]

The past constrains the judge in an extensionalist theory of adjudication but it is the past which is interpreted as a whole and in light of current perceptions of what constitutes the best society. Extensionalism "begins in the present and pursues the past only so far as and in the way its contemporary focus dictates."[27] It seeks to continue the story that previous legal history has begun but its guiding aim is to create "an overall story worth telling now."[28] Judges certainly will not agree upon precisely what story is worth telling now, or share a vision of the best society. Consequently, two judges operating from this methodological perspective could easily disagree over the preferable interpretation. Beyond a certain threshold of fit, substantive ideals of justice, fairness, and due process will determine the best interpretation. Indeed, if an interpretation is far preferable substantively, according to this theory, "it may be given the benefit of a less stringent test of fit for that reason."[29] Far from making narrow consistency with earlier precedents paramount, this form of jurisprudence "encourages a judge to be wide-ranging and imaginative in his search for coherence with fundamental principle."[30]

It should be apparent from this brief description that extensionalism avoids making a radical split between the descriptive and the evaluative components in the activity of interpretation. Although distinguishing between the dimensions of fit and substantive ideals, it acknowledges that these two factors are unavoidably intertwined. The process of determining what the law is is neither mechanical nor objective if that means all judges will read off the identical meaning. The recent legal history of interpreting the meaning of the Equal Protection Clause demonstrates this fact. Unavoidably, the political and moral assumptions of the judge will provide the lens through which the law is viewed. While this does not constitute subjectivism, it does call into question the fact/value dichotomy upon which conventionalism depends.

Given the role that moral and political ideals play in shaping the best interpretation of the past, one might well ask why the past should place any constraints upon the judge's decision. In other words, why should a judge not decide a case solely upon the basis of what will yield, according to his or her moral lights, the optimal society? What possible grounds are there for being constrained by past decisions that may limit one's ability to make the wisest decision in the current case? This is the question that the instrumentalist theory of adjudication relentlessly poses to both conventionalism and extensionalism. According to the instrumentalist style of reasoning, judges should "always look to the future: to try to make the community as good and wise and just a community as it can be, with no essential regard to what it has been until now."[31]

Even though instrumentalism refuses to let the past necessarily delimit judicial decisions, this approach concedes that there may be strategic reasons for taking the past into account. Seeking to avoid societal chaos, the judge should not make rules that stand in direct opposition to other laws which he or she cannot overrule. This strategic limitation to the judge's creativity, however, remains consistent with the fundamental criterion of instrumentalism which is to facilitate the emergence of the optimal society.

To counteract the instrumentalist position, extensionalism must refute the charge that it is irrational to allow the past to have more than a pragmatic role in shaping judicial decisions. To defend the extensionalist's use of the past, Dworkin distinguishes between two ideals that must guide adjudication: (1) an external ideal of a just, perfect society and (2) an internal ideal of the political order of the existing society fairly applied to all members.[32] According to the instrumentalist framework, an individual has no right to expect the latter ideal to be upheld by the courts. Take a case in which a mother is seeking emotional damages for witnessing the death of her child. A judge of the instrumentalist persuasion might reasonably choose to deny such damages, even if they have been routinely granted to others, on the grounds that a better community would result if emotional damages were not awarded. According to the assumptions of extensionalism, the mother has the right to expect the existing political order to be fairly applied in her case.[33] Thus the judge should take into account the fact that such emotional damages have been awarded in the past. This fact will carry more than strategic weight in the decision.

The three models of jurisprudence that Dworkin identifies, then, reflect very different practices and perceptions regarding the role of the past in judicial interpretation. Summarizing these differences, Dworkin writes:

> [Extensionalism] denies that statements of law are either the backward-looking factual reports of conventionalism or the forward-looking instrumental programs of legal pragmatism. It insists that legal claims are interpretive judgments and therefore combine backward- and forward-looking elements; they interpret contemporary legal practice seen as an unfolding political narrative. So [extensionalism] rejects as unhelpful the ancient question whether judges find or invent law; we understand legal reasoning, it suggests, only by seeing the sense in which they do both and neither.[34]

Conventionalism advocates a model of judicial interpretation which, among other deficiencies, is philosophically incoherent. It operates as if the judge could follow authoritative precedents without engaging in complex acts of interpretation that reflect his or her own political and moral proclivities. Instrumentalism, on the other hand, cannot be faulted for a similar kind of incoherence. It does not entail a necessary denial of the general constraining power of the past in shaping human life and thought. However, instrumentalism can be faulted, Dworkin contends, not only for failing to provide an adequate account of judicial interpretation but for failing to recognize some of the moral and political advantages that attend the extension of an "unfolding political narrative." We have to turn now to consider the relevance of Dworkin's exploration of forms of jurisprudence for theology.

Forms of Theological Argumentation

Dworkin's typology of judicial interpretation helps to sort out methodological alternatives in theology, not least by virtue of its distance from the heat and controversy that attend methodological debates within theology. Although not precisely analogous, the methodological roles of the past are parallel in jurisprudence and theology. Applied to theology, Dworkin's typology helps break down the misperception that the theologian's choice is between a heteronomous appeal to past authorities or a forward-looking indifference to tradition. Such a dichotomous perception of the methodological functions of the past in argumentation fails to detect a third alternative lurking between these. Ferreting out this third alternative is important for several reasons. First it makes clear that theological reflection rooted within a particular tradition need not be construed as a confessional or authoritarian form of reflection. Contrary to the charge of some of its critics, then, the contextual nature of theology does not necessarily constitute a form of parochialism that precludes its status as public argumentation. Secondly, the identification of this third alternative not only clarifies and supports the distinction between parochialism and contextualism, but it constitutes an argument against those theologies that continue to follow a "conventionalist" form of argumentation. Finally, the delineation of this third form of interpretation offers theologians highly critical of confessional, dogmatic theologies an alternative to a pragmatic theology with little incentive to engage in an interpretation of the tradition as a whole. The thread uniting these various points, however, is the thesis that this third alternative, extensionalism, constitutes a form of public argumentation, especially suited to the task of theology: the interpretation and extension of a religious worldview.

As we have seen, the first type of judicial adjudication, conventionalism, looks to the past to determine if any legitimate authorities have ruled upon a similar case, whereupon it is constrained to follow relevant precedents. This style of argumentation corresponds to a not uncommon mode of theologizing in which positions are based upon references to designated authorities. Scriptural passages, doctrines, or in certain instances, ecclesiastical pronouncements are invoked in support of a given theological position.[35] Unlike extensionalism that seeks to interpret the tradition as a whole, in its best light, this form of theology takes isolated elements of the tradition as privileged and unassailable. These theological givens are authorities in the strong sense: like legal precedents they constrain the theologian to follow suit in narrow conformity to the past.

Appealing to authorities in this fashion has certainly not disappeared from contemporary religion or theology, despite the continuing criticisms, particularly by the academy, of this form of dogmatics. One need only look to the resurgence of the new Christian right to confirm the prevalence of this theological mode. Nor is it restricted to forms of fundamentalism, as a look at Latin American liberation theologies can attest.[36]

This style of theological reasoning, whether from the left or the right of the political and religious spectrum, is clearly not a form of public argumentation. Although seeking to secure a public impact, these movements often refuse to engage in the forms of open inquiry and persuasion that constitute public reflection. Making this criticism of fundamentalism, Neuhaus rightly notes that "while their message is public in import, it is not public in the sense of being accountable to public reason."[37] "Their reasoning, such as it is, is circular: first accept the truth and then you will know it is true."[38]

Although Neuhaus suggests that this parochial form of reflection is a peculiarly modern phenomenon, other theologians including, for instance, Edward Farley, Van Harvey, and Gordon Kaufman argue that it has been a characteristic of much classical Christian theology, although a characteristic that has only become highly visible and problematic in modernity. In his detailed reconstruction of early Christianity, for instance, Farley contends that theologians operated within a "house of authority," taking certain doctrines and texts as authorities which the theologian presupposed rather than

defended.[39] Classical Christian theology was largely biblical
commentary precisely because of the belief that Scripture was
the revealed Word of God. Hence basing theological positions
on selected biblical passages was entirely reasonable given
prior assumptions concerning Scripture's truth and legitimate
authority. In a similar vein, Harvey draws a sharp contrast
between the "ethic of belief" that informed traditional
Christendom and the modern ethos which celebrates autonomy, skepticism, and sound judgment. Much twentieth
century theology, Harvey contends, reflects a failed effort to
reconcile traditional Christian beliefs with the new ethos that
champions open inquiry.[40] Gordon Kaufman, too, argues that
Christian theology has traditionally been authoritarian in
its mode of argumentation, and understandably so because
theologians "took the basis of their work to be the very word
or words of God."[41]

Although much classical Christian theology may appear
now to reflect a conventionalist approach, this is to some
extent a function of no longer sharing traditional assumptions
concerning the Bible and revelation. Within the classical
framework much theologizing is better accounted for through
the extensionalist model. That is, regardless of the stated
theological criteria, theologians were engaged in an effort to
extend their tradition by wrestling with internal anomalies
and challenges from the wider culture, with the result that
strict continuity with past authorities was not sustained.
Indeed as Kaufman notes, despite the authoritarian model
to which theologians have long given lipservice, their work
"is (and always has been) a creative activity of the human
imagination seeking to provide more adequate orientation
for human life."[42]

There are then complicating factors that preclude a neat
identification of classical theology through this modern
typology. No doubt one could use the typology to discern
tendencies toward each of these types of argumentation in
patristic or medieval theological texts. Whether one takes
classical theology to be largely illustrative of a conventionalist
mode of argumentation or considers that conclusion an
anachronistic reading of much historical theology is largely

irrelevant to the contemporary issue of appropriate argumentation. Within the modern context a conventionalist form of theological argumentation constitutes a parochial form of reflection that isolates privileged authorities from the past and thereby places questionable constraints on theological inquiry and reconstruction.

The increasing attacks upon the authoritarian tendencies within theology, by external critics and some practitioners, make it especially important that greater clarity be reached concerning the appropriate role of the past in theological reflection. A defense of a nonparochial engagement with tradition is needed not only to answer external critics but to respond to theologians who assume that instrumentalism is the only available alternative to the conventionalist mode of argumentation. It may also contribute to a greater consensus concerning the serious deficiencies with the conventionalist approach. We need to turn, then, to an exploration of the extensionalist form of argumentation in a specifically theological garb.

The extensionalist mode of argumentation, like conventionalism, affirms the importance of continuity with a tradition. However, the continuity it seeks is not a narrow consistency with isolated elements of the tradition, but with the principles of that tradition interpreted as a whole. Furthermore, the current insights and values of the theologian are critically involved in this process of interpretation. The theologian does not stand outside the tradition or inhabit some neutral, objective plateau from which to interpret. On the contrary, the interests and values of the theologian are themselves intimately involved in the process of discerning the fundamental principles and insights of the tradition. Moreover, because the story the theologian seeks to tell is one "worth telling now," he or she may legitimately sacrifice the strictest continuity in order to articulate a more adequate story.

An example will help demonstrate the practical import of these divergent hermeneutics. Consider the issue of theological attitudes toward women, specifically, say, in regard to the ordination of women. A conventionalist Christian theological argument might rest its case on the fact that Jesus, the purportedly paradigmatic priest, was a male who chose male disciples.[43] This historical fact resting upon scriptural authority may be extracted out of the past for use as a warrant in the argument against female ordination.

An extensionalist counterargument would need to account for and undermine the fact of male discipleship by considering it within a much broader context. To this end, such an argument might contend that: (1) the patriarchal character of first century Palestine made male discipleship the norm; (2) historical research discloses women were active disciples of Jesus but were written out of New Testament historical accounts; (3) Jesus' overall attitudes and actions toward women counteract the cultural disvaluation of women, thereby functioning as judgment upon continued sexist oppression; (4) the biblical message as a whole asserts the equality of all people under God and hence takes precedent over distortions which inevitably crept in to limit such equality. My point is not to suggest that any of these strategies is determinative, but to identify the sort of wider considerations that are demanded by the extensionalist appeal to the past.

Although not surprising, it is noteworthy that feminist theologies routinely reject the conventionalist mode of argumentation. Given the numerous instances in the Bible and the corpus of theological writings where sexist images and values have been sanctioned, the push to interpret facets of the past within a broad context is readily understandable. This is even true for conservative feminist theologians, as is evident, for instance, in the argument developed by Virginia Mollenkott. She writes:

> Because patriarchy is the cultural background of the Scriptures, it is absolutely basic to any feminist interpretation of the Bible that one cannot absolutize the culture in which the Bible was written. We must make careful distinctions between what is "for an age" and what is "for all time."[44]

In making such a distinction between "for an age" and "for all time," Mollenkott is bringing her substantive ideals of justice and equality to bear in her interpretation of the Scriptures. She concludes that "we are in error to absolutize anything that denies the thrust of the entire Bible toward individual wholeness and harmonious community, toward oneness in Christ."[45] Rosemary Ruether argues a similar position in her work *Sexism and God-Talk*. Although the Bible contains ideological distortions of patriarchy, she claims it also contains a more central thrust that undermines such distortions. In her words:

> Feminism, in claiming the prophetic-liberating tradition of Biblical faith as a norm through which to criticize the Bible, does not choose an arbitrary or marginal idea in the Bible. It chooses a tradition that can be fairly claimed, on the basis of generally accepted Biblical scholarship, to be the central tradition, the tradition by which Biblical faith constantly criticizes and renews itself and its own vision.[46]

Ruether, therefore, attempts to isolate the critical liberating dynamic within the Scriptures and extend it beyond its original applications, arguing that such a move is entirely consistent with the meaning of the prophetic ideal. Through the extension of the prophetic-liberating motif to the oppressive situation of women, the Bible, correctly interpreted, can indeed function, Ruether argues, as a liberating power.

Clearly, the methodological moves operative in both Ruether's and Mollenkott's positions correspond to the moves within an extensionalist theory of adjudication.[47] The interpreter has certain substantive beliefs and moral ideals which shape the interpretation of the past. This is not to suggest that the past is fabricated by the interpreter, but it is to acknowledge that what is deemed important and central will be determined in large part by the interpreter's current beliefs and values. This dialectic is unavoidable given the nature of interpretation, conventionalist denials notwithstanding.

What is at stake here, however, is a methodological self-consciousness about how the past functions in theological argumentation. The extensionalist approach deliberately attempts to interpret the tradition in the best possible light. This entails making judgments, according to one's current perceptions about truth and value, about this tradition. In this case it is not isolated scriptural statements about women that must be addressed finally but the Christian tradition more generally as it relates to the current quest for women's equality. Conventionalist theological argumentation, whether for or against women's equality, which rests upon isolated scriptural references or ecclesiastical decisions will not be considered adequate inasmuch as such warrants are isolated elements wrenched from the total fabric of the past and enthroned as authoritative.

It is interesting to consider in the light of Dworkin's typology Elisabeth Schüssler Fiorenza's criticisms of the methodological moves reflected in Mollenkott's and Ruether's feminist retrievals of the tradition. In her important work *In Memory of Her* Schüssler Fiorenza argues against the adequacy of a feminist hermeneutic which depends upon distinguishing the essential from the nonessential, the form from the content, or the eternal truth from the historical variables in Scripture. Through such distinctions feminists have attempted not only to uncover and reject the patriarchal dimension of Scripture but to rescue the text through the identification of its true or proper meaning. According to Schüssler Fiorenza, such feminist hermeneutics reflect what she calls a "neo-orthodox" orientation which confers an unwarranted authority upon the biblical texts. Instead of granting revelatory status to Scripture, Schüssler Fiorenza argues that a feminist hermeneutic must be more radical in exposing the androcentric character of the biblical writings. These writings, taken singly or as a group, reflect the patriarchal biases of the individual authors and the church that produced and canonized them. Instead of distinguishing Scripture's revelatory kernel from its patriarchal husk, Schüssler Fiorenza insists that women must move behind the text to a historical reconstruction of the life situation from which the texts emerged. The patriarchal texts do not mirror the historical and social context from which they came but offer a selective and perspectival picture of the early Christian communities. As Schüssler Fiorenza demonstrates through historical reconstruction, women can move beyond the silences and backlashes against women found in the Scriptures to an awareness and appreciation of the partici- pation and leadership of women in the life of the early Christian communities. The scriptural portrait of women in the early Christian movement is the "tip of the iceberg"; "what is necessary is a systematic interpretation and historical reconstruction able to make the submerged bulk of the iceberg visible."[48] Only a movement behind the text can enable women to retrieve their heritage, and see their Christian foresisters not merely as victims but as victims and participants in the struggle for liberation.

Although Schüssler Fiorenza rightly distinguishes her feminist hermeneutic from the "neo-orthodox approach" characteristic of Mollenkott's and Ruether's positions, her categories mask the fundamental similarities of these feminist alternatives. From the perspective of Dworkin's typology, her position must be included within the exten- sionalist type. Far from disagreeing with this approach, Schüssler Fiorenza is, rather, attempting to apply its method more rigorously. We have seen that this hermeneutical style rejects conventionalism for extracting isolated bits and pieces of the past rather than for interpreting it as a whole. Schüssler Fiorenza's argument can be construed similarly, as a criticism of feminist hermeneutics that do not adequately interpret the past "as a whole." By resting with suspicion and retrieval of a text, such feminist hermeneutics are neither radical enough in their suspicion of the androcentric texts nor able to retrieve the heritage of women which lies behind the texts. Schüssler Fiorenza, therefore, is not rejecting the extensionalist approach but making very important contributions to an adequate understanding of what is entailed in interpreting the past "as a whole."

At this point it is necessary to consider once again the instrumentalist perspective regarding the role of the past, although this time within the context of theology. If one self- consciously brings current beliefs and ideals to bear in

arriving at the best interpretation of the past, what possible
rationale is there for allowing the past to limit in any way
the most adequate theological vision that can be imagined
for the present? Is it not simply irrational to allow past
interpretations to determine, in more than a strategic way,
the most adequate interpretation in the present moment?
This is the more serious challenge facing any theology that
grants the past a constraining role, even with the modifications that extensionalism introduces. If it cannot be answered
satisfactorily, it makes it difficult to consider extensionalism
an appropriate methodology for a public theology.

In jurisprudence, as we have seen, the justification for
requiring a decision to "fit the past" is based upon the concept
of the political order. Extensionalism argues that this order,
rooted in a long legal history, should be applied to all persons
equally even if it is not exactly equivalent to one's conception
of the ideal political order. But how does this methodological
rationale apply to theology? Although lacking an exact
equivalent to a political order, theology, I shall argue, includes
an analogous notion which justifies common methodologies.
If the aim of constitutional law is both to extend fairly the
existing political order and to improve that order, what might
be the aim of theology? Although we cannot pursue this
question at length, it is through a consideration of the task
of theology that the rationale for an extensionalist model of
theology becomes most apparent.

The Task of Theology

The theologian, I would suggest, is primarily involved in
investigating the meaning, truth, and power of the religious
worldview(s) that shape human experience. This understanding of theology builds upon a considerable body of recent
work in philosophy, anthropology, and sociology, among other
disciplines, which has explored the symbolic construction of
human experience. It has become commonplace to speak of
the interpreted character of experience, to recognize that
human life is shaped by the symbols and myths of a particular
culture.[49] In Clifford Geertz's influential formulation, a culture
embodies a system(s) of symbols that constitute a worldview

and an ethos: a picture of the way things truly are and an emotional and moral sensitivity that corresponds to this picture.[50] Following Ernst Cassirer and Suzanne Langer, Geertz maintains that humans require a symbolic order to orient themselves within the flux of experience. Lacking the instinctual drives that direct behavior, they rely upon these external cultural codes to supply a coherent universe within which they can meaningfully live. These cultural symbolic horizons are not static givens but are, rather, products of human construction that have become fixed in perceptible form. Through ongoing human reflection and activities these horizons continually change. Theology is the discipline that contributes to the interpretation, evaluation and extension of these symbolic universes as they may manifest themselves in a religious mode. This activity is not carried out from a detached, "neutral" perspective but from a practical concern to create a more truthful, meaningful, and powerful vision.

Characterizing theology in this way makes it more difficult to distinguish it from some other pursuits, such as, say, moral philosophy. From my perspective, however, this is an advantage insofar as it avoids some of the increasingly discredited ways of depicting the difference between theology and other disciplines. For instance, to claim that theology is based on faith or revelation and moral philosophy on reason has been undermined by recent methodological studies in both fields. Alasdair MacIntyre persuasively argues in *After Virtue* that the bases for modern moral philosophy lie not in an abstract reason but in a specific view of the human and the world. From this perspective religious ethics and moral philosophy are not differentiated according to their method but according to the differing sources which inform them.[51]

Distinguishing theology from other disciplines by virtue of its object, understood as the sacred or God, is equally problematic in my judgment. The former term is too indeterminate and the latter too parochial for what theology encompasses.[52] Tracy, for instance, defends the role of tradition in theology by appropriating a substantive view of religion as disclosive of the sacred. His theory of a religious classic is an interesting combination of Gadamer's notion of the

classic and the phenomenological portrait of the sacred found
in the history-of-religions school which includes such figures
as Rudolph Otto, Joachim Wach, and Mircea Eliade. According
to Tracy, the importance of the religious classic lies in its
power to disclose a "genuine manifestation of the whole from
the reality of that whole itself."[53] This central claim about
the "manifestation of the whole by the whole" within religious
classics is a metaphorically attractive expression, but its
precise meaning and justification remain unclear to me.
Furthermore, insofar as that is the essential content of a
religious classic (be it event, person, or text) the more
determinate characteristics become secondary, presumably
making it irrelevant which religious classics are addressed.
Instead of pursuing the disclosive power of the sacred within
religious classics, I am developing a different strand within
Gadamer's writings that emerges from his discussion of legal
rather than aesthetic hermeneutics.

Focusing upon a religious worldview as a whole, rather
than upon isolated classics, has two advantages especially
worth noting. First, a holistic perspective more effectively
blocks the conventionalist appropriation of the past which
grants privileged status to isolated elements of the tradition.
My point is certainly not to question Tracy's personal
commitment to sustaining a "hermeneutics of suspicion" in
the midst of the interpretation of the classics, a commitment
which he repeatedly affirms. The question, rather, is which
model more adequately facilitates, indeed encourages, a
holistic, critical interpretation of a tradition. Secondly, the
hermeneutical model that Tracy proposes does not adequately
account for the constructive, creative efforts of the theologian.
There is certainly an element of creativity in all interpretive
acts. But the constructive work of the theologian, in my
judgment, cannot be encompassed within the horizon of the
interpretation of extant classics. Considering theology from
the perspective of extending a religious worldview, on the
other hand, better accounts for the interpretive and constructive poles within theological reflection.

Tracy's systematic theology and the extensionalist model
elaborated above diverge, in part I suspect, because of differing

theoretical assumptions about religion. Underlying Tracy's conversation with the religious classics of a tradition is an understanding of religion as "experiential-expressive," a label that George Lindbeck has helpfully coined to refer to the theory of religion that has come to dominate Western reflection since the early nineteenth century.[54] This understanding of religion has been powerfully expressed, for instance, by Schleiermacher, Otto, Wach, and Eliade, thinkers whom Tracy acknowledges as extremely formative in his own thinking about the nature of religion. As Lindbeck explains, "thinkers of this tradition all locate ultimately significant contact with whatever is finally important to religion in the prereflective experiential depths of the self and regard the public or outer features of religion as expressive and evocative objectifications (i.e., nondiscursive symbols) of internal experience."[55] It may be this understanding of religion that leads Tracy to speak of religious classics as potentially "manifestations of the whole by the whole." This understanding of religion would legitimate the conversation with a classic, without requiring much focus on the location of that classic within a much wider interpretive tradition. The understanding of theology that I am developing, on the other hand, is, again to appropriate Lindbeck's terminology, rooted in a "cultural-linguistic" conception of religion. It construes religion more in terms of a language than an experience, a conceptual framework that is learned rather than an experience that is undergone.

Understanding religion in "cultural-linguistic" terms and interpreting theology as the critical reflection upon and extension of this symbolic framework decisively shapes its methodology. Theology's practical concern to facilitate the emergence of more adequate religious frameworks places particular constraints upon it. To create meaningful and powerful conceptual frameworks is contingent upon their being inhabited. The theologian is not simply creating fictitious worlds that are logically coherent, aesthetically appealing, and morally attractive. Such imaginative construction is the domain of art, literature being a striking example. Ralph Bellamy's *Looking Backwards* and Charlotte

Perkins Gilman's *Herland* are classic examples of the literary imagination envisioning a utopian society in great detail. It is certainly not my intent to deny that such imaginary flights can have enormous impact upon altering our perceptions of reality. Indeed there are good grounds for claiming that literary works play a decisive role in altering our symbolic worlds.[56] Theology, however, does not "start from scratch" to construct more adequate symbolic worlds but starts from a given worldview that has emerged in a specific culture over the span of many generations. Standing within a particular tradition(s) of interpretation, the theologian attempts to extend it in the most appropriate way. The process is akin to the novelist working on the chain novel: to continue the worldview successfully requires that the theologian take account of what has gone before. This does not mean that the theologian (like the novelist) plays no creative role; but it does mean that the creativity is bounded by the demand to go on in continuity with what has gone before (to modify this worldview), rather than to begin from a clear slate. The theologian is, like Michael Walzer's moral philosopher, a "connected critic," one who "enters imaginatively into local practices and arrangements."[57] Continuing an inhabited symbolic universe is not merely a product of conservative tendencies within the profession but a reflection of its central task.

The theological aim to extend a communal tradition with shared memories and expectations receives powerful support, then, from the emerging sense that religion is more like a language than an experience. If religious experience and devotion are not available to the individual except through a tradition of social mediators, consisting of language, texts, and institutions, then sustaining, reforming, and extending the tradition lie at the very heart of the theological enterprise.

Although the metaphor of the chain novel is useful in illuminating both the retrieval and the creativity of the theologian in relationship to a tradition, it is somewhat misleading insofar as it implies that a tradition is monolithic. In continuing a novel one has been given the prior chapters; determinate bounds have been set for what is to be continued.

Obviously the situation is exceedingly more complex in relationship to a historical tradition. It has become a commonplace that traditions are extraordinarily pluralistic, including phenomena which may have dim family resemblances at best. The diversity of a tradition, however, does not invalidate the model so much as it underscores the creative leeway of the theologian and helps account for the plethora of proposals offered as candidates for the chain. For there are many directions to take a tradition, many ways of reading it and extending it; although this does not mean that "anything goes," it does accord a significant role to the critical and creative input of the theologian.

The significant parallels between jurisprudence and theology are now more apparent. While there is no exact equivalent to a political order within the domain of theology, there is an analogous element. The theologian engages a religious tradition, embodied in symbols, texts, and practices, which he or she interprets and extends. In this theological model the past certainly constrains the theologian insofar as some degree of continuity is required to write the next chapter. However, the continuity is with the most charitable interpretation of the tradition viewed as a whole, not with isolated authoritative precedents to which the theologian must strictly conform.

There are, however, important disanalogies between theology and jurisprudence as well, especially constitutional jurisprudence. An American judge is appointed to decide cases within a constitutional legal system. The U.S. Constitution is a body of laws that functions as the authoritative basis of the entire legal system. Although a judge can creatively interpret a constitutional statute, he or she is not free simply to disregard it. There is no theological equivalent to this document. Clearly, the Bible, when understood as the revelatory word of God, at times has functioned in theology much like the Constitution functions in jurisprudence. Indeed one still finds the Bible assuming this sort of role in forms of contemporary theology, from more reactionary fundamentalists to very sophisticated narrativist theologians. However, it is exceedingly misleading to accept this analogy without serious qualification. Isolated scriptural passages are not parallel to constitutional statutes that the judge is appointed to uphold. To assume they are is to misconstrue the character and status of the Bible, to take it as a compendium of God's laws for humans. Nor should the Bible taken as a whole be considered, like the Constitution, the definitive authoritative precedent. Although more palatable than fundamentalist literalism, this position fails to recognize fully the human, and therefore corrigible, roots of the text.

On the other hand, when interpreting the tradition "as a whole" it is inevitable that the Bible will figure centrally given the constitutive role of Scripture in the Christian tradition. (This historic constitutive role, of course, is not unrelated to the fact that it was traditionally construed as God's revelation.) This does not mean, however, that the theologian must follow in strict conformity to this isolated text. Unlike constitutional statutes, the theologian can attempt to argue, for example, for the rejection of particular Christologies, divine metaphors, or encoded attitudes toward women or Jews which no longer appear persuasive or appropriate in light of the tradition interpreted as a whole in its best light. Hence, while engagement with the Bible is necessary to write the next chapter of the tradition, this does not give it the role of the Constitution in theological reflection. Indeed the primary danger in using jurisprudence as an analogy for theology is that the important differences between the Bible and the Constitution will be obscured by their genuine and, in an earlier time more prounounced, similarities.

Concluding Remarks

The burden of this chapter has been to identify a model of public theological argumentation. Appropriating Dworkin's typology to explore forms of theological argumentation has served several purposes. By distinguishing between conventionalism and extensionalism in theology, I have attempted to clarify and defend the distinction introduced at the beginning of the chapter between parochialism and contextualism. This distinction is critical to making clear that the choice we face is not between a heteronomous capitulation to the past or the impossible ideal of an ahistorical autonomy freed from its constraining power. There is an alternative to these extremes, one that incorporates the rejection of authorities without resorting to an objectivist, ahistorical transcendence of particularity to ensure this rejection. To acknowledge this alternative is to acknowledge the possibility of a genuinely public theology, reflecting not the Enlightenment construal of public but its historicist reconfiguration.

This argument, however, only got us part of the way. For there are really two choices that remain after eliminating these two extremes: extensionalism and instrumentalism. Their differences are not a function of the opposition between public and parochial. Both, I would suggest, are legitimately public insofar as each aspires to a form of open inquiry. But both are not equally appropriate as modes of public theological argumentation. As I have argued, extensionalism is a more adequate account of the theologian's task. This judgment rests upon a theory of religion that accentuates the social and institutional mediators that are needed in the formation of religious experience, belief, and practice. Belief in and commitment to God, for instance, are only possible because of religious traditions with sophisticated concepts, symbols, and narratives which render this religious orientation a genuine option. To appreciate this point is to appreciate the appropriateness of extensionalism as a mode of theological argumentation. Dworkin's typology of jurisprudence, then, is equally important for uncovering the features and rationale of a form of argumentation especially suited to the maintenance, transmission, and reformation of religious traditions.

To recognize the suitability of an extensionalist form of argumentation to the interpretation and extension of inhabited religious traditions does not require that the instrumentalist option be eliminated. Certain circumstances, certain ages may lead the theologian to construe a tradition as so bankrupt or distorted that continuing it is deemed morally and intellectually unacceptable. (Again, the theologian differs from the judge who is appointed to interpret the reigning political and legal order.) But it is important to notice the possible costs and perhaps unintended consequences of this choice. Generally speaking, the less continuity that is sustained with a tradition, the less impact one will have upon those that inhabit that tradition. The irony is that instrumentalism in theology may actually function conservatively to reinforce the status quo. For though the theologian him- or herself may proffer a radical vision, its very lack of continuity with and impact upon a tradition isolates it, making it personally satisfying for oneself and perhaps a few like-minded colleagues but socially impotent. The very radicality of the voice excludes it as a formative influence in the extension of the tradition. Although this observation can hardly be dignified as a rule, it is especially pertinent to the effort to develop a public theology. It provides added support to the contention that extensionalism is the more appropriate mode of reflection for a theology that is seeking a greater public voice than is a forward-looking eclectic vision with minimal ties to a tradition.

To achieve a public form of argumentation, theologians must make changes on two fronts. On the one hand, they must unmask the impossible pretensions to neutrality and universality that underlie the Enlightenment understanding of public, and the public exercise of reason. On the other hand, they must respect the Enlightenment distinction between open inquiry and dogmatic citation, and work to combat the authoritarian traces that linger on in contemporary theology. Neither of these changes will be easy. For they both cut against the grain of deeply entrenched assumptions and practices. But it is only in and through these changes that theologians can rightfully claim a public voice.

Chapter Three

Toward the Reconfiguration of the Public Realm: The Cultivation of a Common Life

In our project to develop a model for public theology we have concentrated so far upon one of the central characteristics of this kind of theological reflection: its public form of argumentation. As noted previously, however, the concept of public includes several distinct senses, each of which has some bearing upon the nature of a public theology. In this chapter the focus will shift to a different sense of public. Rather than consider the contrast between public and parochial, we will be dealing with the distinction between the public and the private. Exploring this opposition will shed light on the distinctive substantive agenda of a public theology: to contribute on both a practical and theoretical plane to the reconfiguration of public life.

We need to consider, however, precisely what this means. It certainly entails overcoming the modern relegation of religion and theology to the private realm wherein issues of individual religious experience and personal ethics are primary. But this negative characterization of public theology is not sufficient; it fails to specify the nature of the public realm that stands over against the private. I shall argue that the prevailing interpretation of public life is not fully adequate. Hence the substantive agenda of a public theology is not captured in the injunction to move beyond the private sphere. Just as the parochial/public polarity needed to be deconstructed to accommodate a more adequate interpretation of public argumentation, so too the private/public contrast demands revision if we are to develop a much needed sense of public life. Clarifying the substantive task of public theology to reconfigure public life, then, leads us into a consideration of the further alterations in the meaning of public that this agenda entails.

To anticipate, I will argue that the prevailing configuration of the public realm, fundamentally rooted in and shaped by the Enlightenment project, reflects both the genius and the distortions of this historical epoch. On the positive side, it is a vision of public life that has unleashed a powerful universal dynamic and played a critical role in enhancing the autonomy and rights of the individual. In the process, however, this interpretation of the public realm has contributed to a defective construal of rationality, the subject of the preceding chapter. It has also contributed to a growing individualism that has undermined the attitudes and assumptions needed to sustain a flourishing social life, the primary focus of this chapter. The central question at issue concerns the proper reformation of the public realm so as to correct the excesses and distortions of the modern liberal trajectory without sacrificing its significant gains. After exploring the prevailing configuration of the public realm, then, I will consider its strengths as well as its weaknesses in an effort to develop a more adequate alternative.

The Prevailing Configuration of Public Life

The dominant interpretation of the public has been shaped in response to the Enlightenment project with its emancipatory and irenic aims. The religious strife of the sixteenth and seventeenth centuries made it imperative that a "neutral" language be developed that could articulate the nature of society and the individual without recourse to sectarian religious beliefs. In retrospect it is clear that the secular discourse that arose in this context was by no means neutral; on the contrary, it reflected very explicit assumptions about the nature of the individual, society, and rationality.[1] The effort to escape from the control of the established hierarchies in civil, social, and ecclesiastical life fostered a radical individualism that has come, increasingly, to dominate

Western life and theory in the succeeding centuries. By stressing the freedom and autonomy of the individual, particularly in regard to his or her vision of the good, the legitimacy of the entrenched authorities was undermined. Society, according to classical liberalism, is a collection of autonomous individuals with idiosyncratic values and goals. It is not based upon a shared vision of the good nor is it the product of any intrinsic connections amongst individuals. On the contrary, individuals "choose" to enter into a social contract for purposes of security. Government is entrusted with the task of maintaining order, thereby ensuring the protection of the life and property of individuals. Classical liberalism and its ensuing institutional embodiment have had significant ramifications for the configuration of public life. This historical trajectory has fostered a radical individualism that has contributed to the erosion of a communal sense of public life. The very effort to emancipate the individual from the varied chains of "the other," whether embodied in a tradition or a social group, weakened the sense of connection between the self and the other. To augment human freedom and autonomy separation and independence were championed over the relations and dependencies between the self and the other. The consequence was not only a weakened perception of the connections between selves but the gradual erosion of such connections. Public life was not envisioned as an inclusive relational life reflecting some basic shared goals, but as the collective sum of autonomous individuals whose values and goals are resolutely private.

This strategy not only succeeded in fostering human freedom and autonomy, but it reflected the universal impulse that animated the Enlightenment outlook. Expanding the depth and range of the private sphere made room, theoretically if not actually, for a radically encompassing sense of public life. Because diversity was relegated to and legitimated within the private sphere, the public realm could contain everyone—not in terms of a personal biography but in terms of a public persona. And this was identical for all persons, rooted in a common nature or capacity that each possessed.[2]

The result was a sense of public life that was, at least potentially, universal in scope but exceedingly formal in substance. Public life was not a fabric woven out of the myriad relationships and connections between peoples, but the receptacle that contained the individual units. In a very real sense public life in this scenario was the individual writ large, the duplication on the macrocosmic level of its microcosmic atomism.[3]

This model of the public and private realms is based upon their clear distinction and separation. The all-encompassing character of the public sphere depends upon removing private entanglements, the specificities of personal lives. The archi-tecture of nineteenth century America begins to reflect this construal of public and private life, as spaces become clearly designated as one or the other.[4] The latter part of the nineteenth century, for instance, witnesses the establishment of major public spaces such as national parks, zoos, and sports arenas. Similarly the definition, enlargement, and protection of private spaces, most notably the home, become central preoccupations. These developments reflect a gradual change in the value and importance attributed to the private realm. What had formerly been regarded negatively, that is, that which was not public, now takes on an independent and positive valuation.

There is little doubt that this interpretation of the public and private spheres, which continues to structure the social landscape, has yielded great gains. It not only has contributed to furthering and legitimating human freedom and diversity, but it has been a main expression of and vehicle for the universal dynamic of the Enlightenment spirit. I do not want to deny nor minimize the importance of these very real contributions. On the other hand, it is also important to recognize the underside of this way of constructing public and private life, an underside that has only recently become visible to any great extent.

The receptacle model of public life suffers from two main defects. First, it obscures and, gradually, erodes the connec-tions between the members, thereby reflecting and exacer-bating the radical individualism upon which it is based.[5] The controlling assumption, in other words, is that individuals are autonomous beings whose public life is a matter of external association, not substantively shaped by the personal values and ends of the individuals.

Secondly, the receptacle model of public life generates a static, unchanging sense of the public as a fully formed vessel. This point is, of course, an extension of the first defect. The receptacle is given, there, ready to be filled. The sense of nurturing or transforming the public realm makes little sense within this framework. As the collection of the individual units public life is quantitatively configured, not substantively constituted by the concrete particularity of its members. As a consequence, the equality accorded all members of the public realm is exceedingly formal, generated by abstracting the individual from the distinguishing marks of race, gender, occupation, religion, or class. This formal construal of equality can all too easily serve as an ideology that leaves intact the real inequalities that mark social life. "Spheres of economic domination and subordination, exploitation and competition, are left untouched or are buttressed by the notion of a separate political realm in which such distinctions do not figure."[6] Both the individualism and the formal, "ready-made" character of the receptacle model of public life contribute to an inability to recognize a shared public life that demands cultivation and transformation.

Indeed far from thinking of the public in terms of a common life, we are more apt to regard it as a "battleground between divergent self-interests."[7] Not surprisingly, this assumption engenders an understanding of politics as the jockeying for power of special interest groups. What happens when this vision of public life dominates sensibilities, belittling all communal contenders as hopelessly naive or romantic? Given the dialectic between theory and practice, it should come as no surprise when actions assume the shape and tone of their interpretive frameworks.[8] By embracing a "minimal vision of what is possible among people," we "create a dismal self-fulfilling prophecy."[9] The sentiments and motivations that would sustain a sense of common life are obscured and weakened in the face of repeated denials of any substantive basis for it.

Many depictions of contemporary American life have sought to trace just such a trajectory wherein public life is construed more as a battleground for power politics than a common life based upon shared principles and mutual obligations.[10] Although other influences, such as notions of covenant and the kingdom of God, have also shaped American life, these religious motifs have been decreasing in power and influence in the twentieth century. As a result, their tempering of the liberal strain in the dominant ethos has lessened in recent decades, leaving, increasingly, a stark version of liberalism as the primary mythic framework for interpreting social, economic, and political life.[11] Many now take the nineteenth century warning of Alexis de Tocqueville against a virulent individualism that threatened to undermine the American experiment in democracy as prophetic. Following this line, critics, such as Robert Bellah and William Sullivan, have suggested that the individualistic strain in the American heritage has become unleashed from its republican and biblical moorings which, historically, had limited and contained it.[12]

Support for this portrait is garnered from many sources. Perhaps most cited is the emergence of a culture of consumption in twentieth century American life with its resultant narcissistic and materialistic ethos. Marked transformations in behavior and attitudes have accompanied this development. Within, for instance, the Protestant bourgeoisie, once the dominant force in American cultural life, the new ethos has been described as "the shift from perpetual work to periodic leisure, compulsive saving to compulsive spending, civic responsibility to apolitical passivity, Protestant self-denial to therapeutic self-fulfillment."[13] Indeed this portrait would appear to capture a fairly broad range of the American middle class.[14] Burton Bledstein, for instance, connects the transformation to the professionalization of American life producing an ethos which, among other things, has elicited and legitimated preoccupation with an individual's private career path. The resulting focus has been on vertical movement up the professional ladder with its attendant increase in wealth and status. This vertical vision has helped to eclipse horizontal sensitivity, leading its inhabitants to reject "as misfits" those persons who either call for "a horizontal social unity of their fellowmen" or "uncondescendingly merge(d) their identity with the unworthy poor below."[15]

The rather dramatic surge of interest in "spirituality" in the last decade lends further support to this picture of a growing individualism in American life. Consider, for example, the proliferation of interest in the "New Age" religiosity which is fast becoming a major current within popular culture. The professed aim of this diffuse and variegated movement is the cultivation of a new spirituality that will provide for a sense of meaning and connection, purportedly lacking in modern life. By eliciting an experience of wholeness new agers hope to overcome the radical fragmentation and spiritual malaise that they contend plagues twentieth century life. Their growing presence provides further testimony to the conviction that a virulent individualism has taken root in American culture, eroding for many the communal sources for meaning and identity.

There is much evidence to suggest, then, that the radical individualism of classical liberalism combined with the ascendancy of consumerist capitalism have merged to shape an ethos with troubling ramifications for social life.

Beyond Community and Society

The substantive agenda of public theology to reconfigure public life is only intelligible against the backdrop of the historical and social context sketched above. A public theology seeks to elicit a recognition of and loyalty to a common public life that is more than a collection of autonomous individuals. By focusing upon the intricate and extensive interdependencies that mark human and cosmic life, it seeks to temper the radical individualism of the liberal ethos through identification with a wider common life. By cultivating this sense a public theology seeks to sustain, deepen, and transform the common life that has been obscured and deformed within the liberal framework.

To understand the proposed reinterpretation of the public realm it is necessary to move beyond the now common contrast between a community and a society, the alternatives that have tended to structure our thinking about individual and corporate life.[16] Although oftentimes of heuristic value, this dichotomy impoverishes the alternatives that need to be imagined for both descriptive and prescriptive purposes. Community has typically been used to identify homogeneous associations exhibiting extensive consensus in regard to beliefs, values, and ends. The stronger the community, the more extensive and deeply felt the consensus, with intimate, face-to-face relations functioning as the paradigmatic form. Largely developed in opposition to community, society has been construed as a far larger, more diverse association, with impersonal and legal relations serving as the paradigmatic form. In the context of modern pluralistic societies, this heuristic device suggests that the impersonal legal relationship is the only realistic alternative, given the impossibility of achieving wide-scale consensus short of coercion.

This dichotomy between community and society is further reflected in the supposition that we must choose between either affirming a common good or recognizing the privacy of values and ends. The former alternative, of course, reflects the tradition of communitarianism and the latter the liberal tradition concerning individual and corporate life.

The proposed reinterpretation of public life, reflecting ties to both of these orientations, depends upon charting a path that moves beyond their oftentimes polemically driven form.[17] My aim is to formulate an alternative which avoids the atomistic and ahistorical propensities within liberalism as well as the homogeneity and exclusivity of communitarianism. It is important to make clear that this project is not an effort in restorationism. Communitarian critiques of the liberal vision of self and society often suggest that we need to return to some state of affairs that existed prior to the dawn of the modern era. Earlier ages are exalted for their communitarian form of life within which individuals shared similar values and ends. This idealization of premodern life rightly recognizes the communal context of individual identity and action, but it is a form of romantic nostalgia when its drawbacks are silently passed over. Although a strong communal identity existed in many social forms prior to the modern era, this identity typically arose within small kinship or tribal associations. The unity and intensity of communal life that existed within the local unit were complemented by fragmentation and hostility between these smaller associations. Furthermore, the sense of belonging that such communal life made possible sharply curtailed the freedom, privacy and rights of the individual members. Thus the kind of communal life that existed in the premodern world is neither possible on a large scale today nor indeed desireable.

The conditions of modern life make both possible and necessary a different form of public life. We are at a stage when our sense of public life, although incorporating local and national identities, must include a global thrust. Obviously such a public life precludes basing it upon the intimate face-to-face relations of smaller groups. It also precludes making it a function of an extensive agreement about the values by which or the ends for which we live. Any public life dependent upon such a consensus is either a figment of the utopian imagination or an Orwellian nightmare.

But we are not limited to choosing between public life as the atomistic collectivity of liberalism or the unified life of a homogeneous and intimate community. This study is proposing an alternative option: an understanding of the public realm as an all-encompassing common life that embraces substantial diversity—in regard to values, beliefs, and behaviors—amongst its members. Such diversity, however, does not go all the way down.[18] The assumption that it does, it seems to me, is a peculiarly modern reading of the situation. To counteract this reading I propose to distinguish between a common good and a common life, the former reflecting the moral consensus of a community and the latter the interconnected relational web that provides the indispensable basis for all individual pursuits. This distinction, if successful, goes a long way toward illuminating and defending the proposed reconfiguration of public life.

Revising the Liberal Narrative

In order to clarify and defend the proposed distinction between the common good and a common life, it is necessary to reconsider the liberal narrative through this contrast. The liberal tradition that has placed such a strong emphasis upon the freedom and autonomy of the individual continues to draw its power from a deeply rooted sense that we do not share common values and ends. To counteract this rendition of modern society, which reinforces a merely contractual sense of public life, it is essential that this intuition be accounted for if not undermined. This is no small task for it is an intuition that appears to be confirmed in innumerable ways in contemporary life.

Consider, for instance, the raging dispute over the issue of abortion with its intertwined religious and ethical dimensions. Opponents of abortion often base their position upon the assumption that a fully human life begins with the moment of conception, an assumption that is usually the product of a particular religious ontology. Those advocating free choice often do not share such an ontology, and hence have no compelling reason to restrict a woman's control over her own reproductive life. The power of the liberal tradition lies precisely in its ability to account for this kind of dispute. Recognizing the divergence in religious and ethical orientations, the liberal tradition construes them as "private" options. Moral and policy debates over issues as diverse as homosexuality, pornography, and capital punishment provide similar ammunition for the liberal framework. This evidence appears to be clear and unmistakable support for liberalism's solution to the relationship between the individual and society. Unless this evidence for the diversity and privateness of values and ends can be accounted for in an alternate explanatory framework, efforts to recognize a common public life, united by some shared ends, will lack persuasive power.

Without denying the diversity of the values and ends not only within but between cultures, it is worth considering whether we have become blind to some important commonalities that underlie the differences. By construing values as private options of autonomous individuals are we ignoring aspects of our life that are shared by others, values that are essential to the survival and flourishing of us all, goals that we share despite the obvious and important disagreements amongst us? In other words, underneath the differences that divide us are there commonalities, that are significant not trivial, that we have ignored, devalued, and perhaps diminished as a result of our preoccupation with the freedom and autonomy of the individual?[19] If an affirmative answer to this question can be convincingly made, as I think it can, then efforts to cultivate a communal sense of public life assume a credibility, perhaps even an urgency, that they would otherwise lack. We have to consider, then, what values and goals individuals embrace that require for their attainment the existence and nurturing of a common life.

The Social Nature of the Self

One of the recurring insights of modern philosophy and psychology involves the social nature of the self.[20] Theorists have largely abandoned substantive theories of the self in favor of ones that emphasize its social and temporal character. No longer conceived of as a substantial entity entering into external relation, the self is considered to be radically constituted by its relations. Rather than possessing an enduring essence or identity, the self is a dynamic process of creation and re-creation. The self seeks to "become itself" by interpreting its chaotic experiences into some significant pattern. The self is constituted by a narrative that provides a structure and meaning to the otherwise disparate moments and events of its life. Becoming a self, then, is an ongoing project that entails the interpretation of one's past and future, thereby producing the coherence and identity that distinguish the self from the biological organism.

This process of becoming a self is not carried out in isolation. That is, a self does not invent for itself the narratives by which it will create the necessary pattern and meaning for its life. On the contrary, the self inherits the narratives of specific communities which become the interpretive lenses through which the individual self is fashioned. We are, in other words, thoroughly shaped by the cultural traditions into which we are born. These traditions supply the metaphors, rules, principles, images, and stories through which and by which we construct our particular narrative history. Individuals do appropriate these traditions in distinctive ways, sometimes in very creative ways. This element of creativity, however, does not nullify the self's fundamental reliance upon such cultural resources without which the individual could not even initiate the process of forging a coherent, meaningful self.

If the above account of the social nature of the self is generally correct, then it establishes an important connection between the individual and society. If the self is constituted by its relations, and dependent for its identity upon cultural narratives, then we can begin to glimpse the deficiencies in classical liberalism.[21] From this vantage point the autonomous self of liberal theory is an abstraction from the relational web within which the self is formed. The autonomous self is surreptitiously wrenched free from its familial, social, and political relationships. The neediness of the self vis-à-vis society goes far beyond the safeguarding of personal property and life. The individual self needs others for the most basic task of becoming a self. Thus the dependence of the self upon society is inadequately reflected in social contract theories that presume the existence of selves prior to their real or imagined choice to enter into social relations.

Recognizing the social nature of selfhood constitutes a small but important first step in the reconstruction of the liberal narrative. Highlighting the social relations and historical traditions that constitute the self exposes the mythic exaggerations to which the liberal narrative is prone. But it clearly does not get us very far. For the social nature of the self does not stipulate what kind of social life, or indeed what kind of cultural narratives, are needed to forge a coherent, meaningful self. It is obvious that many forms of social life have supplied the contexts within which integrated, meaningful identities have been nurtured. Individuals can and have taken as their primary communal contexts their extended family or tribe or, more recently, nation. Indeed in our own time recognition of the social nature of the self has been used as a defense of sectarian enclaves that can mitigate the chaos of competing stories within a pluralistic culture by offering a single coherent narrative for the patterning of the self. Given the global sense of public life that I am seeking to elicit, it clearly is not simply deducible from the social nature of the self. In order to move from the minimal social setting within which selfhood is possible to a cosmopolitan public life, compelling reasons for the adoption of a more inclusive communal context must be articulated.

The Social Nature of Knowledge

One reason for embracing a communal context more inclusive than tribe, sect, or nation emerges in and through a recognition of the social nature of knowledge. Although this point is more controversial and complex than the following can suggest, I do want to sketch out briefly the connection between the commitment to truth and to more inclusive community. Recognizing this connection furthers the argument in two ways. First, if the relationship between truth and community can be substantiated, then the fallacy of relegating values and ends to the private realm receives further confirmation. Secondly, establishing the link between truth and community helps to clarify and support commitment to a global sense of public life. From this angle it is possible to see that public life need not depend upon complete consensus about the truth, but in sharing the commitment to the pursuit of truth.

The social character of knowledge has grown more visible in the wake of recent philosophical attacks upon correspondence theories of truth.[22] If knowledge were a simple correspondence with reality, in theory it would be possible for the individual to achieve such correspondence in isolation. Whether the recipient of reliable sensations or intuitions, the individual could presumably discern what is the case apart from any interaction with others. Recent emphasis upon the linguistic character of our knowledge of the world has radically undermined any confidence that we can achieve knowledge independently from others. This "linguistic turn" underscores the perspectival character of all knowledge, the recognition that our grasp of the other is always dependent upon our social and historical location. Knowledge is not a simple ahistorical correspondence between idea and reality but the product of a cumulative interpretive process. Social consensus is an important facet of this process, functioning as both the ground and the lure. However, the role of power in shaping agreement, and the open-endedness of this process preclude making truth simply a function of consensus. Nevertheless, its role in the formation of knowledge makes it apparent that the pursuit of truth is not an end that the individual can achieve alone; it is fundamentally and inescapably a social process. It demands the presence, nurturing, and extension of a common life wherein inquiry, conversation, and critique can take place.

The possibility of any knowledge at all presupposes the presence of some social consensus, some set of shared meanings and assumptions. The existence of a common language is the most obvious manifestation of such a consensus; it constitutes the vehicle in and through which individuals engage their world. This basic level of agreement oftentimes goes unnoticed as the strident disputes extending from the empirical to the moral realm capture our attention. But disagreement, to be disagreement and not sheer incommensurability, cannot be total. Far from being simply "other," it is powerfully shaped by the prevailing view in the very act of distinguishing itself from it. As Walzer remarks in regard to contemporary philosophical disputes, they are not "a mark of social incoherence." On the contrary, "these are highly ritualized activities, which bear witness to the connection, not the disconnection, of their protagonists."[23]

Although playing an indispensable role in the pursuit of truth, social consensus clearly cannot be equated with truth or taken as its definitive marker. To do so would be to ignore an important facet of the concept of truth. Although what now enjoys a social consensus is dignified by the designation "knowledge," or "truth," we recognize a difference between that which is shared according to current lights and that which is valid "in the long run," as a pragmatist might say. Consider the claim that the earth is at the center of the universe. At one time, of course, this claim was taken as axiomatic. With more sophisticated instruments and motivation for empirical observation, evidence emerged to undermine this claim and dissolve the consensus that it enjoyed. In turn the heliocentric model of the universe gained ascendancy.

More and better empirical evidence, however, is not the only factor with the potential to disrupt the social consensus currently operative. It is equally important to consider the way in which power shapes knowledge, thereby producing a "consensus" which is coerced. The writings of Marx and Foucault, among others, have helped to expose the ways in which socially accepted views are forged and legitimated through channels of power that are controlled by the few. The social consensus that determines what passes for knowledge at any given time, then, often depends upon ignoring or silencing whole segments, identified, for instance, through class, race, gender, or species, which lack the power to make their perspective and interests heard.

Positing an "ideal social consensus" that functions as the goal toward which the interpretive process moves preserves the critical principle built into the concept of truth. Such a consensus is clearly an imaginative construct, a regulative ideal in Kantian language. For some the sheer impossibility of such a goal makes references to it problematic. Despite its potential to mislead, articulating such an ideal performs important functions with regard to our understanding of truth. Most importantly, reference to an ideal social consensus is able, simultaneously, to acknowledge the social character of the pursuit of truth without reducing it to any extant consensus. Furthermore, this imaginative construct calls attention to the moral component in truth seeking, a component which has been all too hidden by the empirical turn. We have been too ready to link truth with "getting the facts straight," thereby obscuring the way in which power and privilege contribute to shaping the construal, selection, and arrangement of the facts themselves. In short, linking truth with an ideal consensus underscores the need for attending to all perspectives which through neglect or coercion have not contributed to the social conversation.[24]

Rather than pursue what could easily become a very complex and extended discussion on the nature of truth, let me connect the above observations with the larger effort to articulate the substantive agenda of a public theology. My all too brief remarks on the social nature of the quest for truth are aimed, primarily, at exposing the distortions that liberalism's public/private grid creates in our understanding of an end such as truth. Although individuals must certainly cultivate personal moral and intellectual qualities in the pursuit of truth (i.e., honesty, capacity for self-criticism), it is not an end that is intelligible in terms of the autonomous individual. It depends, rather, upon the presence, nurturing, and extension of a common life wherein inquiry, conversation, and debate take place. Such a common life is not the product of a complete and final consensus on the truth, but of a limited, provisional one whose presence is obscured by the noise and emotions that attend disagreements.[25] Moreover, given the "transcendent" dimension to truth—its critical function vis-à-vis our current insight—commitment to truth instills in the current level of common life a loyalty to an ever expanding common life wherein "complete mutual under-standing" may be realized.[26] This goal is obviously not realizable within the historical process but its reference highlights the intimate connection between truth and the presence and extension of a community of inquiry, apart from which the quest for truth is unintelligible. To be committed to the pursuit of truth, then, is to be committed to the cultivation and extension of a common life that is, at least hypothetically, radically inclusive in its scope.

Survival in the Modern Age

Whatever cogency remote excursions on the communal conditions of knowing may have, they possess little power to revise the prevailing paradigm. As Richard Rorty has aptly remarked, "One would have to be very odd to change one's politics because one had become convinced, for example, that a coherence theory of truth was preferable to a correspondence theory."[27] A more immediate and, no doubt, more compelling motive to revise the liberal narrative has emerged in and through the conditions and capabilities of the modern age. It has become increasingly apparent that not just human flourishing, but survival itself, is dependent upon the creation of some sense of common life that tempers the narrow loyalties that define us. Without the emergence of such a global identity the technological advances of modernity threaten to destroy the fabric of life that supports all of our proximate values and goals. The power unleashed through modern technology, in other words, has dramatically altered our situation making both possible and imperative a new cosmological-moral vision.

It is the emergence of nuclear warfare in the twentieth century, of course, that has altered our situation most fundamentally and created the most urgent need for a form of global identity. The destructive technological capability of nuclear weapons has made exceedingly clear the dangers of the reigning political structures and their identity forming power. The system of nation-states is much too volatile and divisive to forestall for very long the redeployment of this weaponry. This has become newly apparent in the wake of the rapid disintegration of a centrally controlled Soviet Union which has thrown a wrench into theories of deterrence. Our technological advancement has outstripped our political, moral and religious development. The nuclear crisis that now confronts us establishes the need for a global identity that defuses the nationalisms that threaten to unleash a nuclear holocaust. The modern age with its nuclear capabilities provides a compelling reason for the cultivation of a public life that includes and yet transcends the narrow communal contexts as the primary settings for individual identity.

The preceding observations concerning truth and the nuclear crisis underscore the relationship between the survival and flourishing of the individual and a larger common life which requires continual nurturing and extension. The common life that these reflections on truth and the nuclear age call attention to can easily be construed as a community of humans dedicated to the pursuit of truth and the creation of a just interdependent international order. This anthropocentric interpretation of our common life, however, is seriously defective. It has become increasingly apparent that the industrial and technological advancements of the modern age have created an ecological crisis of overwhelming proportions. Indeed we are only beginning to recognize the extent to which our actions have interfered with the earth's ecosystem. Unless we learn to acknowledge and respect the interconnected web of life that binds us resolutely together, we appear destined to harm irreversibly the environment within which we exist, thereby imperilling not just other life forms but our own.

It is largely in light of the ecological crisis, then, that the deficiencies in locating human loyalty and identity within a universal human community become most visible. The challenge we face is in developing a sense of common life that goes beyond the shared identity of a human association, however extensive. Moving in this direction depends upon overcoming the tendency to regard a community that is more encompassing than the human species sheer romanticism or nature mysticism. It depends, in other words, upon a paradigm shift in our understanding and evaluation of the natural order. This process has clearly begun, reflected in a growing recognition of the intricate ties that bind life forms into a complex interactive field. But the deeply rooted assumption that the natural order is the constant backdrop for the human drama is not easily eliminated. As one writer, speaking from the emerging science of climatology, observes:

> A stand of timber isn't simply inert, out there to be used; it is part of the community, maintaining it and to be maintained by it, to ensure the continued existence of both. We don't have that conception of our atmosphere. It exists outside of human society—a constant. We breathe it, fly through it, dump waste into it, use it—and it is simply there. The same is true of the oceans, of rain forests, of groundwater, and so on. The natural world is an arena in which our individual aspirations, as people or nations, have had unlimited play.[28]

Rather than continue to regard the physical world as radically "other," we need to recognize the intimate interdependence of all life forms that constitute a reciprocating field. In this model actions of any one have a ripple effect throughout the whole. It is from this perspective that not only the legitimacy but the urgency of recognizing a common life becomes most apparent.

Cultivating a sense of common life that is more inclusive than the human species will depend upon the transformation of our macrocosmic visions that provide the overarching patterns for perceptions, sensibilities, and behaviors. Thomas Berry, one of the most articulate advocates of the ecological movement, contends that piecemeal tinkerings within our current worldview are not enough to transform our destructive behaviors and attitudes. A much more radical revolution is needed: "Our challenge is to create a new language, even a new sense of what it is to be human. It is to transcend not only national limitations, but even our species isolation, to enter into the larger community of living species."[29]

The nuclear and ecological crises within which we find ourselves, crises arising from the technological developments of modern life, clearly expose the deficiencies, indeed horrors, of narrow communal loyalties that lack a universal thrust. In the contemporary age it has become painfully apparent that neither family, tribe, nation, nor humanity supplies the appropriate communal context for human life. Only a commitment to a radically inclusive common life can now ensure our respective survival and flourishing. It is this point especially that makes the recent turn to community problematic. Turning inward to more cohesive, homogeneous associations all too easily loses sight of the newly emergent moral mandate to create some form of global association that can relativize our strident nationalisms and temper our anthropomorphic proclivities.

But the push toward a more global, inclusive sense of common life is not without its own dangers. Given the prevailing interpretation of public, especially, a more global identity can easily be construed in antithesis to local associations and their respective traditions. There are good reasons for thinking, however, that abstractly defined collectivities merely pave the way for totalitarianism, the flip side of an exaggerated individualism. As Walzer succinctly puts it, "The more dissociated individuals are, the stronger the state is likely to be, since it will be the only or the most important social union."[30] Our challenge lies in the struggle to discern and create a form of common life that avoids the twin perils of an autonomous individualism or a simple collectivity that is ripe for totalitarian control. Meeting this challenge, in my judgment, depends upon forging a construal of public life that incorporates a global thrust without thereby sacrificing local sources of meaning and identity. It is to the elaboration of this reconception of public life that we now turn.

Toward the Reconfiguration of Public Life

The above explorations into the nature of the self, truth, and survival raise some fundamental questions about the adequacy of the prevailing vision of public and private life. My aim has been to uncover certain ends that we share, or should share, regardless of the very real differences that divide us on specific moral, political, and religious issues. Focusing upon these ends, as opposed to moral controversies like abortion or capital punishment, generates a very different picture of the social landscape. We can begin to see the distortions that the prism of liberalism creates in its exaltation of freedom, creativity, autonomy, and diversity. Although extremely successful in fostering the freedom and rights of the individual, and in accounting for the moral stalemates that mark modern social life, in the process this tradition has obscured, and slowly eroded, the commonalities that sustain human life and flourishing.

This does not mean, of course, that the liberal tradition has been simply mistaken in its rejection of a common vision of the good that all people share irrespective of their social and historical location. We clearly do not agree on all of the specifics that constitute the good life. This holds not just across cultures but within any given society, as even a cursory glance at our social, moral, or political conflicts will demonstrate. Recognizing the limitations in the classical liberal perspective does not mean, then, that it is wrong on every count. It does mean, however, becoming more aware of the exaggerations and silences this historical trajectory has perpetrated in its pursuit of emancipation and enlightenment. We have become especially blind to the intricate ties that bind us with one another, and with the whole of the created order. To overcome this myopia we must become attuned to the very real sense in which we share a common life that is indispensable to our quest for selfhood, truth and, especially in our time, survival.

A driving force behind the reconfiguration of the public realm is the recognition that the self is not intelligible as an autonomous being but is essentially constituted by its relationships, both near and far. With this reinterpretation of the self as fundamentally social, the receptacle model of public life loses intelligibility. In its place it is necessary to reconceive the public realm as the whole fabric of interrelated beings whose specificity is not outside public life but the substantive texture of it. With this reconfiguration the stark disjunction between the private and the public collapses. Although there remains an essential place for the private realm, it can no longer be construed as an inviolable sphere that remains insulated and isolated from a wider social arena.[31] In other words, instead of an abstract public realm set over against a concrete, substantively specific private realm we have a configuration of public life that is constituted by the interests, values, and projects of its inhabitants.

An important corollary of this reconception of public life is the recognition that it does not exist ready-made, like a container that remains constant despite changes in its contents. This recognition brings with it the realization that the equality of an abstractly constituted public life is an eviscerated equality that all too easily turns an indifferent eye to the relations of domination and subordination structured by economics, race and gender. Moving beyond a formal equality entails abandoning the quantitative construal of public life upon which it is based.

Overcoming the reigning polarization between the private and the public makes clear that individuals play a critical role in shaping the substance of public life and, conversely, that public life does not just externally include individuals but forms them as well. This insight is essential if we are not only to account for but to place greater weight upon the responsibility of individuals in sustaining and reforming a shared public life. Dworkin's defense of an extensional model of jurisprudence, what he calls law as integrity, illuminates this realignment between the private and the public. His reasoning on this issue is worth considering at some length, not least because it underscores the correlation between the proposed reconfiguration of the public realm and the earlier reconception of public argumentation that occupied us in chapter 2. In defending an extensional model of judicial interpretation, that is law as integrity, Dworkin recognizes that it depends upon linking the moral and the political more closely, thereby overcoming the sharp separation between the private and the public realm. He writes:

> Integrity infuses political and private occasions each with the spirit of the other to the benefit of both. This continuity has practical as well as expressive value, because it facilitates the organic style of change I mentioned a moment ago as a practical advantage. But its expressive value is not exhausted, as its practical value might be, when citizens disagree about which scheme of justice is in fact embedded in the community's explicit political decisions. For the expressive value is confirmed when people in good faith try to treat one another in a way appropriate to common membership in a community governed by political integrity and to see each other as making this attempt, even when they disagree about exactly what integrity requires in particular circumstances. Political obligation is then not just a matter of obeying the discrete political decisions of the community one by one, as political philosophers usually represent it. It becomes a more protestant idea: fidelity to a scheme of principle each citizen has a responsibility to identify, ultimately for himself, as his community's scheme.[32]

In the realignment between the public and the private realms that follows from law as integrity, individuals clearly have more than a quantitative relationship to public life. Membership in a public realm goes beyond numerical impact to include an unmistakable substantive role in the interpretation and extension of this realm. Individuals, in other words, have the responsibility to interpret their public order with its varied traditions and current problems critically and holistically. It is this process that collectively and through time sustains, reforms, and extends a common public life whose vitality and health are closely correlated with that of its inhabitants.

The closer alignment between the private and public realms that Dworkin advocates rests upon an understanding of public life that underscores its particularity. For Dworkin public life is not some abstract whole but a particular historical order constituted by an interlocking complex of institutions, laws, principles, events, and narratives. It is a self-consciously historicist construal of the public realm. This point becomes especially important in light of the emerging moral mandate to cultivate a more global identity. It guards against the supposition that a global identity is most adequately achieved by transcending from local cultures constituted by a rich tapestry of common events, laws, narratives, and institutions. As we will consider further in the concluding chapter, a global public life must not be developed by abstracting from public life as it is exemplified in various cultural units, but by reformulating them from within.

Metaphors, Myths, and Theology

The problem with liberal theory is not simply that, as a caricature, it is an academic theory that does not quite fit the social landscape. The more serious problem is that classical liberal theory has come to assume a mythic hold over the American imagination, molding behaviors, attitudes, and values to fit its image. The "fit" grows increasingly more secure.

The power of language, metaphors, and myths in the formation of selves and societies frequently has been noted of late by scholars within the humanities and social sciences. As Clifford Geertz has expressed it, "Becoming human is becoming individual, and we become individual under the guidance of cultural patterns, historically created systems of meaning in terms of which we give form, order, point, and direction to our lives."[33] Mythic frameworks generate particular discourses which, far from being mere rhetoric, frame the experiences, conflicts, and questions of the moment. The liberal caricature is problematic insofar as it has become the mythic vehicle for a vision of the human and society with increasingly deleterious effects.

Approaching classical liberal theory in terms of a cultural myth not only illuminates some of the debates between contemporary liberals and their critics but it points toward the sort of revisioning that is especially needed today. It is not uncommon to hear contemporary liberals rejecting the liberal picture painted by its critics. As Will Kymlicka has noted regarding the standard picture of liberalism, "it's remarkable how often this accepted wisdom gets passed on without the least bit of textual support."[34] To undermine the accepted wisdom he explores the interpretations of the self developed by John Rawls, a contemporary liberal, and Michael Sandel, a communitarian, concluding that the differences are largely "apparent."[35] While Kymlicka provides a strong defense of contemporary liberal thinkers, his analysis sheds little light on the reasons for the current misunderstandings and controversies. Recognizing classical liberal theory as a culturally dominant myth, with textual roots in seventeenth and eighteenth century philosophical treatises and political tracts, makes the "standard picture" far more understandable. It also accounts for the failure to attend carefully to the contemporary philosophic variants of this tradition. For it is not Rawls the contemporary liberal philosopher but the culturally embodied myth of liberalism that is at issue.[36]

The proposed reconfiguration of public life constitutes an effort in mythic revisioning with the aim of modifying the liberal tradition not abandoning it. It is with this goal in mind that I have focused upon the importance of recognizing, nurturing, and expanding a common life rather than upon acknowledgement of a common good as the basis of moral community. There are several reasons for adopting this tactic. Retrieving the notion of a common good, with its particular historical associations, risks at this moment in time the misperception that we share a detailed and final consensus on the good. To preserve the truth of liberalism's insight into the reality and value of moral diversity, it may be wise to avoid the slogan that suggested otherwise. It is possible, of course, to modify the notion of the common good so as to avoid the monolithic and ahistorical connotations that it bears.[37] Indeed the position I have developed could be translated, with the appropriate modifications and cautionary footnotes, into discourse about the common good.

But even with the necessary qualifications, the notion of the common good fails to capture the intricate maze of interconnections that relate us one to the other. It does not go far enough, it seems to me, in combating the individualism and the anthropocentrism of our prevailing vision. It suggests a human consensus about the good, a rational agreement that can too easily be divorced from the natural world within which humans are embedded. Attending to a common life, by contrast, forces us to include within our frame of reference the interconnected web of life upon whose well-being we are so completely dependent.

By extension, attention to this inclusive common life makes it easier to underscore the perils that attend its betrayal or deformation. The rationalistic tenor of the notion of common good can block awareness of the actual repercussions that attend the failure to realize it. In other words, not acting for the common good can be assimilated to a personal moral failing, the wider ramifications of which are left in the background. Recognition of a common life whose survival and well-being are intricately connected to our own, however, more clearly ties human flourishing to that of the wider cultural and natural life of which it is a part.

Revisioning public life as an interconnected web, or common life, rather than a receptacle containing isolated individuals clearly reflects a macrocosmic perspective that attends to the overarching metaphors and pictures which shape thoughts, sensibilities, and behaviors. There are those, certainly, who would find this perspective irrelevant, too vague and abstract to be useful in addressing the serious moral dilemmas that we confront. This level of discourse is significantly different from, say, moral reflection upon particular case studies. It has in many respects been eclipsed as the analysis of moral dilemmas has become the dominant paradigm in contemporary ethical reflection. There is good reason to think, however, that too much attention is directed to those moral quandaries which yield no easy solution.[38] Most of our behavior and attitudes flow unself-consciously from basic root metaphors through which we interpret human and cosmic life. Hilary Putnam, for instance, calls these root metaphors "moral images of the world," rightly noting that moral philosophers today prefer to traffic in specific duties, rights, principles, or virtues rather than in these larger, amorphous pictures. The problem with this move to greater specificity is that it often fails to attend to the overarching visions that shape sensibilities and interpretive stances out of which the intellect and the will operate. As Putnam notes: "millions of human beings have found in those metaphors moral images that could organize their moral lives—and this notwithstanding the enormous problem of interpreting them and of deciding what it could possibly mean to make them effective."[39]

One of theology's more important tasks today is in keeping alive the tradition of attending to the "metaphysical-moral" visions by which people live.[40] Although not a replacement for "moral reflection within the trenches," its wider angled lens is an indispensable tool in cultural critique and moral transformation. Without it, we are too apt to limit our conversation and debate to choices that do not challenge the fundamental assumptions and values of the dominant paradigm.

Rorty's recent work which explores issues of public and private life suffers, I think, from his failure, or rather refusal, to adopt what I would call a macrocosmic perspective. His refusal reflects his conviction that the public and private spheres cannot be united, and theories that seek to bring them together in any overarching perspective are failures. As he puts it, such theories "ask us to believe that what is most important to each of us is what we have in common with others—that the springs of private fulfillment and of human solidarity are the same."⁴¹ Considering this belief a metaphysical or theological fiction, Rorty suggests that we allow each sphere its own autonomy and regard "the demands of self-creation and of human solidarity as equally valid, yet forever incommensurable."⁴² Some writers, then, are experts at illustrating "what private perfection—a self-created, autonomous, human life—can be like."⁴³ Other writers are concerned with making our public institutions more just. We do not need, nor can we create, a theory that unifies these incommensurable pursuits. Indeed to seek such a theory is, for Rorty, an indication that one has not sufficiently negotiated the historicist turn, in other words, that one continues to "believe in an order beyond time and change which both determines the point of human existence and establishes a hierarchy of responsibilities."⁴⁴

Much is compelling about Rorty's position, a modern variant of the liberal tradition. He is certainly right that no theory can ever provide one with a blueprint for knowing when to seek, in his language, private perfection and when to work towards justice. And he is also right, I think, to deny the identity between private perfection and human solidarity, the assumption that their separate pursuits fully overlap. But does this mean that we ought to accept a radical disjunction between the private and public spheres? What are the repercussions from separating our exploration of private perfection and the public good? For fear of fusing the public and private spheres, Rorty insists upon their incommensurability. But this tactic simply exacerbates our current inability to recognize the ways in which our private pursuits *are* linked with a common life. Failure to appreciate their overlapping attracts us to visions of private perfection that are if not self-defeating from a holistic perspective, too easily insulated from their wider destructive effects. To escape this myopia we need to move away from the assumption that we are radically autonomous beings whose private perfection can be construed within some isolated sphere. Fear of fusing these two spheres should not preclude explorations of their interconnections and overlappings.

At this point we are in a better position to understand the substantive task of a public theology. To say simply that such a theology engages issues and problems of public life is not sufficient. For, as we have seen, the public realm is like a chameleon, absorbing and reflecting the color of its surroundings. The configuration of the public landscape that we have inherited is built upon the artificial atomism and ahistoricism of the classical liberal vision. Although still exceedingly powerful, and once exceedingly liberating, this tradition needs transformation now that it has gone from the margins to the center of our cultural life. We need to cultivate a sense of the public realm that is based upon the thoroughly relational character of the web of life whose nurturing and transformation holds the key to our own survival and well-being.

The task of a public theology is to elicit a recognition of and commitment to the common life within which we exist. In and through the appropriation of religious symbolism, public theology seeks to nurture, deepen, and transform our common life that, while obscured and damaged, is never totally eroded. Thus public theology is not simply proposing a utopian communal vision that flies in the face of what we know about cosmic and human life. It is, rather, offering a constructive agenda that grows out of discernible features of our individual and corporate experience. But why engage religion, and more especially theology, in the project to cultivate a more inclusive, relational sense of public life? The sectarian impulses and divisions that attend religion might initially appear to make it a hindrance rather than a vehicle for this project. After all, it is commonly recognized that religions all too often create factions that disrupt rather than unify social life. While true, this is not the whole story.

There are a number of reasons, both pragmatic and substantive, for engaging religion in the effort to sustain and transform public life. From a purely pragmatic but nonetheless important perspective, religion constitutes a form of discourse that continues to command significant meaning and power within our culture. The prophets of secularization of recent decades appear to have been premature in their

prediction of the demise of religion. The continued vitality
of religion, globally, suggests that modernity does not necessarily bring with it a decline of the religious life.⁴⁵ Whether
or not, as some suggest, we are witnessing its dying gasps,
religion in our own time continues to grasp the minds and
hearts of the majority of the inhabitants of the modern world.
This means, first, that religious imagery and symbolism
continue to be meaningful and intelligible to the vast
majority. Just as importantly, however, it means that religious
discourse retains substantial power to motivate human life.
This is particularly significant for a public theology that is
concerned not just with defending but with actualizing a more
interconnected and interdependent sense of public life. To
escape the hold of the liberal caricature, a meaningful and
empowering revision must be forthcoming. The argument
advanced thus far which has sought to expose the limitations
in the liberal vision has, if successful, merely opened the door
to a transformed sense of public life. It has not, however,
offered a constructive alternative with the mythic power, both
intellectually and emotionally, to effect such a change.
Religion retains such power.

However, the rationale for appropriating religious discourse
in this project goes beyond merely pragmatic considerations.
In other words, there are substantive religious reasons that
point toward the proposed revisioning of public life. I suspect
that a number of religious traditions offer resources for such
a project, hence the possibility of a Jewish public theology,
an Islamic public theology, or indeed one rooted in Native
American cosmological and ritual life.⁴⁶ I will not argue this
point here, however. My concern is more modest: to identify
from a Christian perspective the correlation between monotheism and the proposed reconfiguration of public life.

Engaging religion in this project becomes all the more
compelling when contemplating other alternatives, or more
properly put, the absence of alternatives. I am not aware of
alternate traditions of discourse in our culture that can
generate a recognition of and commitment to the radically
inclusive, relational public life proposed herein. From this
perspective, then, the role of religion and theology in the

reconfiguration of public life is not just justified but indispensable.

Although arguing that Christianity has resources for contributing to the upbuilding of public life, I would not thereby deny alternative trajectories within the tradition that have either ignored or actively undermined a sense of common life. One need only point to some types of mysticism which concentrate attention upon personal religious experience or to forms of sectarian Christianity that have primarily sought to provide a critical distance or a safe haven from "the world." One must also note that Christianity has in recent centuries accommodated itself to the privatization to which the modern world has relegated it. Hence in many respects Christianity has recently functioned more as religious legitimation to the dominant worldview rather than as a challenge or alternative to it. Nevertheless, I think it remains true that an important trajectory within the Christian tradition, and one that needs to be retrieved in our own time, offers the resources and the rationale for cultivating an inclusive, relational reconfiguration of public life.

A Christian theology that contributes to the upbuilding of a public life will need to focus attention upon the symbol of God, what Gordon Kaufman has aptly called the anchor symbol for an entire worldview.[47] My observation borders on the platitudinous since few would deny that God should hold center stage in any Christian theology. My sense, however, is that the development of an interpretation of God constitutes the central agenda of a Christian public theology, displacing such foci as ecclesiology, Christology, or anthropology. Obviously the latter topics are inextricably interwoven with interpretations of God's nature and activity. They also can be the lens through which a comprehensive theological vision is fashioned. Nevertheless, such topics can easily overshadow theological reflection upon the divine reality. Because it is primarily in and through an excavation of the meaning of God that the religious basis and rationale for an inclusive common life emerge, a Christian public theology will focus primary attention upon the nature and activity of God. I cannot develop this topic to any great extent within the parameters of this work. But I do want to suggest the general outlines of an interpretation of God that, in my judgment, facilitates the development of a Christian public theology. It is to this task that we now turn.

Chapter Four

God and Public Life

In the preceding two chapters we have explored the reigning interpretation of public, considering its historical roots and contemporary manifestations. The cogency and influence of this interpretation, I have suggested, are a reflection of the cultural dominance of the "myth of liberalism" in contemporary American life. In the previous chapters I have attempted to sketch out an alternative interpretation of public, considering its ramifications for rationality and argumentation, on the one hand, and the nature of public life, on the other. But it is one thing to identify deficiencies in a mythic rendering of experience and another to offer an empowering alternative to it. How can the sense of common life advocated in the previous chapter be elicited, particularly given the continued vitality of the reigning liberal ethos? It is here, especially, that theology can play a critical role in the reconfiguration of public life.

The question we shall tackle in this chapter goes to the heart of the project to develop a public theology: how might the symbolism of God lend itself to the cultivation and transformation of public life? I deliberately put the issue in this way in order to avoid intimating that commitment to God necessarily elicits a concern for a public life. It certainly does not. It is quite apparent that belief in and devotion to God can be interpreted in ways that do little to cultivate a loyalty to a larger common life. Consider existentialist theology or popular evangelical piety in American life in which the emphasis upon the personal relationship of the individual to God has dominated. But there clearly are other dimensions to the symbolism of God which, far from mirroring the modern individualistic trajectory, call it into question in important

98   *Religion, Theology, and American Public Life*

ways. They have been submerged precisely because of their incompatibility with the modern ethos. Retrieving these "lost" dimensions is critical to the development of a vision of God with the power to modify rather than merely reinforce the liberal paradigm.

It is clearly impossible to develop, let alone to defend, a comprehensive interpretation of God in the confines of a single chapter. But my interest lies less in comprehensiveness than in the critical points of contact between monotheism and the proposed reconfiguration of public life. My primary agenda is to make clear that commitment to God, properly understood, is not neutral with respect to interpretations of the public realm. On the contrary, a central dynamic of monotheistic faith, I shall argue, leads toward the reconfiguration of public life proposed herein.

To limit what could easily be a much more extended discussion, I shall develop an interpretation of God in terms of God's traditional roles as creator, sustainer, and redeemer. Proceeding in this fashion makes it easier to identify both the continuities and the discontinuities between this vision of God and more traditional formulations. Underscoring the continuities is especially important to avoid the impression that this effort in constructive theology is simply an arbitrary manipulation of traditional symbolism for the contemporary purpose of modifying the liberal worldview. That kind of functionally driven theological creativity is seldom persuasive. But even more importantly, such a theological strategy fails to expose the substantive affinities that link the proposed interpretation of God with its historical antecedents.

Affirming the substantive correlation between monotheism and the proposed reinterpretation of public life does not depend upon ruling out contemporary influences in their respective formulation. The preceding chapter identified some of the historical and technological developments of recent centuries that have made this interpretation of public life not only possible but necessary. Similarly, the following interpretation of God is also responsive to modern insights, both moral and scientific, that differentiate it from more classical formulations. Reflecting Dworkin's model of extensional jurisprudence, the following interpretation of God includes both forward-looking and backward-looking moments, each critical in the endeavor to sustain and extend the narrative coherence of a particular religious worldview. Identifying points of contact between monotheism and the proposed reconfiguration of public life not only constitutes a theological defense of this reconstrual of public life, but it challenges sectarian theologies that fail to carry through fully the universal implications of monotheism.

The critical importance of monotheism to the revisioning of the public realm, I shall argue, arises from both its onto- logical and normative dimensions, emphases that can be distinguished although not neatly separated.[1] From an ontological perspective, the relationship of God to the whole of the created order provides the basis for the common life that lies at the heart of this revisioning of public life. But the universalism of this ontology incorporates a powerful normative trajectory as well. For commitment to God generates more than a recognition of the reality of a common life; it provides both definition and motivation for the struggle to nurture, deepen, and transform it. The ontological and normative dimensions of monotheism merge most fully in the universal community of being, the eschatological vision toward which this struggle is directed.

Monotheistic faith, then, provides powerful support to the foregoing reinterpretation of public life not only by directing attention to the reality of a common life but by generating an ethic that endeavors to nurture and transform this life. Throughout this discussion we will have to consider how these two functions are related. At least initially, there is some tension if not contradiction between recognizing a common life and building one. Recognition presupposes the reality of the object, while building presupposes that the object needs to be created or transformed. As I shall argue, however, these activities are not contradictory but dialectically related, each constituting an important moment in the ongoing project to sustain and transform public life. How to understand God's role in relation to each of these moments will be of primary concern. For the danger is that God will be understood in relation to one moment only, thereby undermining rather than facilitating the cultivation of the public realm.

God as Creator

The central Christian affirmation of God as creator of all that is must be retained and underscored in a Christian public theology. Historical and scriptural study make clear that God's role as creator of the heavens and the earth has dominated Christian consciousness throughout the ages. In our own time this emphasis upon the cosmological activity of God has receded, due largely to the emergence of scientific explanations of the origins and development of life that contradict, in various ways, the biblical portrait of creation. The impact of science has led to a deemphasis upon God's relationship to the cosmos and an increased focus upon the relationship between God and humankind, fostering the tendency to construe issues of spirituality, ethics, and salvation in very individualistic terms. There is a considerable price to pay for moving in this direction. By downplaying the role of God as creator, we risk cutting the relationship between God and the cosmos as a whole. Not only are we left with a very anthropocentric deity, but it becomes increasingly difficult to see God as more than a human projection. I would suggest that modern scientific developments require us to revise, but not abandon, the Christian affirmation of God as creator.

There is no doubt that modern science has falsified many of the mythological details through which affirmations of God as creator have been expressed. It would be less anachronistic to say that modern science has required us to distinguish between scientific and mythological interpretations of the cosmos. By forging this distinction we have come to recognize that many of the details comprising our mythology of creation are not just scientifically unfounded, but indeed false when judged from the vantage point of science. For example, that the earth is only 6,000 years old, or that humans were created before other forms of life, or that God created according to the six days or epochs identified in Genesis are claims that cannot be taken as literally true in light of what science has shown us about the origins and development of life. But does this rule out completely an understanding of God as creator?

So long as science does not help to explain why there is something rather than nothing, the religious interpretation of creation remains viable, perhaps compelling. The increasing success of the sciences in identifying the processes through which life has developed has blinded us to their failure to account for the presence of life at all. As Ludwig Wittgenstein once noted, the most mystical moment consists in contemplating why there is something at all rather than nothing. This fundamental religious question is simply by-passed, not answered, by scientific explanations of how life develops.

Although scientific explanations need not preclude a recognition of God as creator, they do contribute to our understanding of what this means. The mythological portrait of creation in Genesis, for instance, has long fostered the tendency to place humans at the center of the divine creation. The rest of the natural order has served, then, as a backdrop against which the divine/human drama is played out. This sort of anthropocentric interpretation of creation loses plausibility in light of recently acquired knowledge about the evolution of life. We in our post-Darwinian world are hard put to see why we, as one species among so many others, are the center or rationale of the created order. Quite the contrary, evolutionary science, extending the trajectory of the Copernican revolution, has compelled us to recognize the continuities between human life and other forms of life. This trajectory has displaced humans from center stage, forcing us to recognize our embeddedness within the whole network of cosmic life. Contemporary affirmations about God as creator, then, must leave behind the anthropocentric frame of reference that typically characterized earlier formulations. We just cannot continue to regard the human species as the raison d'être of the created order, with other life forms largely props or tools for our use and enjoyment.

But why continue to speak of the world in terms of a divine creator? Simply escaping scientific prosecution is not sufficient reason for preserving this affirmation. To appreciate the importance of this motif it is necessary to look more closely at the sensibilities and values that it sustains. Speaking in terms of the creator God, as noted above, is the vehicle for a basic mystical wonder about the presence of life itself. A variety of sensibilities associated with this primal response can be identified. From the mystical moment emerges the religious intuition that being itself is a gracious gift, something we cannot secure but can only accept. Through this theological rendering of ontological wonder, a sense of connection to and dependence upon the creative life force is both cultivated and expressed.

A theistic interpretation of the ontological moment, moreover, plays a critical role in sustaining the sense that life itself is meaningful. Rather than being the chance result of chemical interactions onto which meaning is projected, a created universe gives "ontological roots" to meaning. In other words, it is somehow in the nature of things, far wider and deeper than the imaginings of the human species. This ontological grounding helps to temper the modern idealistic trajectory that has tended to emphasize, indeed overemphasize, the constructed character of our symbolic worlds, thereby slighting their touchstones in reality. Affirmation of a divine creative source not only anchors meaning in the nature of things, but it valorizes the whole of the created order making possible the recognition of a common public life. From the perspective of the creative source, the worth of beings is not simply a function of whatever momentary value they may be judged to have by one of the many beings within the manifold. We are most apt, of course, to make the self or our own kind, family, tribe, or nation, the lens and standard by which we interpret and value the rest of the cosmos. Even modern ethical theory which extols its universal perspective routinely appropriates the human species as the measure of morality. A divine creative source offers a basis of value that is not calculated solely in terms of its value for any individual, group, or species. It forces moral reasoning to at least begin with the presumption that the various life forms have a prima facie claim to survival and well-being within the created order. Although the tragic and predatory character of life force relative judgments of worth to be made, this initial religious presumption instills a critical reverence for all life forms.

H. Richard Niebuhr, perhaps more than any other modern theologian, has provided the clearest and most persuasive case for the importance of this theological motif. As he has argued, a radical monotheistic faith both relativizes and lends value to all that is. In his now classic formulation of this orientation he explained: "As faith, it is reliance on the source of all being for the significance of the self and of all that exists. . . . It is the confidence that whatever is, is good, because it exists as one thing among the many which all have their origin and their being, in the One—the principle of being which is also the principle of value."² Commitment to God, to the principle of being, means that no finite reality can be considered absolute. Monotheism, therefore, is radically iconoclastic; by focusing upon the power of life by which being is it relatives the realm of being, recognizing the equal dependency of all being upon this life force.

On the other hand, radical monotheism does not generate an indifference to being as a result of its commitment to the principle of being. Rather, loyalty to the power of life that informs all being occasions the valuation of and loyalty to the realm of being. God, the power of being itself, is misconstrued if regarded as a being over against the realm of being. On the contrary, as the power of being itself, God is the life force that makes being possible. Faith in and commitment to God, therefore, elicit a respect for the whole of being.

At this point we are in a better position to recognize some of the critical links between monotheism and the interpretation of public theology advocated herein. Insofar as theology devotes primary allegiance to exploring the reality and significance of God, surely true for Christian theologies if not their post-Christian descendants, it must faithfully reflect the universal dynamic that is rooted in and expressed through God as the creative source of all that is. This means, first, that nature cannot be viewed as the devalued arena within which the history of human salvation plays itself out. On the contrary, nature is valorized as the human is re-situated within the interconnected web that constitutes the cosmic order.

The universalism in the symbolism of God has profound implications in the social arena as well. Although a theology is always a reflective exercise emerging within a particular discursive tradition, monotheism precludes making any extant community a closed horizon within which meaning, purpose, and value are calculated. Although it will become clearer in a consideration of God's role as redeemer, the divine mandate is not to create an oasis of salvation within a larger fallen world but to work toward the transformation of the whole. To undercut this universal thrust of the divine life is to operate with a tribal deity whose primary interest is in the life and welfare of a particular people.

The universalism at the heart of monotheism is subject to its own insidious distortions, as the global histories of theism clearly reveal. It is an impulse that slips easily into imperialistic behavior against "the others" who may worship other deities or none at all. It is a troubling question as to whether the logic of monotheism ineluctably spawns this darker trajectory. Whatever the historical verdict on this issue, it is possible to identify an alternate strand within monotheism that counteracts this imperialistic proclivity. Affirming a divine creative source to the created order implies that other perspectives have value and integrity. From this angle, monotheism functions more as a vehicle of tolerance and respect for alternate interpretations of the cosmos than as a weapon for their destruction.[3] It may be that this interpretation of the universal impulse within monotheism has had to await the rise of historicism before its full power and significance could be tapped. Earlier interpretations of monotheism have tended to emphasize the believing community's possession of the truth, divinely revealed through scripture and creed. Within this authoritarian framework, universalism functions more as instigation for getting "them" to recognize the universal truth that "we" have been given. The rise of historicism, however, may unleash this alternate

dynamic within monotheism which, far from validating
imperialistic behaviors, provides critical support for the
recognition of a radically inclusive common life that recognizes that the pursuit of truth depends upon engagement with
all perspectives, none of which can be peremptorily dismissed
out of the conviction that truth is fully possessed.

My argument thus far is that the affirmation of God's role
as creator serves important theological and religious purposes, many of which provide a basis for the proposed
reinterpretation of public life. Insofar as this affirmation is
not falsified by modern science, it warrants continued assent.
As I have suggested in this brief sketch, recognition of a
creator God elicits an acknowledgement of and respect for
a comprehensive life which includes and valorizes all beings.
This is an indispensable element in the proposed revisioning
of public life. However, it is not sufficient. There is a real
danger of distortion when God's role as creator is affirmed
in isolation. Without belittling its continuing power to
articulate significant religious intuitions about the cosmos,
one must also recognize the limitations of this symbolism.
It is an exceedingly abstract or timeless way to envision God's
relationship to the cosmos. It functions much like a snapshot
in its emphasis upon the dependency of all life forms upon
the creative source. Such a static portrait fails to capture the
diachronic character of the creative life force. In other words,
God is not simply creator in an abstract sense but creator
of this order with its particular forms of life and development.
God's roles in sustaining and redeeming creation seek to
capture this historical facet of the divine activity, thereby
offering important correctives to the symbolism of God as
creator.[4]

Failure to recognize the limitations in the symbolism of
God as creator runs the risk of misconstruing the status of
the common life that monotheism engenders. Emphasizing
God's role as creator in isolation from God's roles as sustainer
and redeemer too easily suggests that the community of being
is a given reality, albeit only visible from the divine perspective. It too easily suggests that the mere fact of existence
reflects the extent of the divine intentions. Such a religious

interpretation validates the status quo. By redirecting attention from the created order with its tragedy and discord to the community of being, fully constituted by virtue of the divine source of all being, it encourages an uncritical embrace of what is. It falsely presumes that the community of being is a product of a transformation of vision, rather than a transformation of reality. To safeguard against this misunderstanding it is necessary to consider God's roles as sustainer and redeemer, particularly as they bear upon an understanding of the nature and status of the universal community of being.

God as Sustainer

Consideration of God's role as sustainer directs attention to the ordering and direction discernible within cosmic reality. By focusing upon the divine sustaining activities, the tendency to abstract the creative moment from its particular place within the created order is minimized. God is not, as deism would have it, the creator now withdrawn from the created order, but the ongoing creative and ordering processes within cosmic life. This emphasis temporalizes the creative role, locating it within an ongoing directional process. It downplays the mere fact of existence through its emphasis upon the development of cosmic life. The tendency to regard the community of being as an extant reality, visible from monotheistic eyes, is minimized. Neither, however, does this emphasis render the community of being simply an ideal goal, with no touchstones in reality. Neither fully given, nor fully future, the community of being is a work in progress when viewed from the vantage point of God's roles as sustainer and redeemer of cosmic life. Although only a shadow of its ultimate form, it is a common life that is manifest in the interconnectedness of cosmic life and most vividly confronted through the consequences that follow from the failure to acknowledge and respect it.[5]

Before pursuing these implications of God as sustainer, however, we must consider, if only briefly, how this role can be affirmed in a contemporary theology. References to the divine role in providing order and direction to cosmic reality trespass upon the terrain of modern science in a way that affirmations of God's role as creator need not. Indeed the conflict between religion and science in recent centuries has been instrumental in forging the modern, liberal strategy that isolates these realms, regarding each as legitimate but distinctive language-games. The cost for pursuing this "apologetic strategy" has been exceedingly high.[6] Interpreting religion as a distinctive language-game has contributed to the cognitive devaluation of its substantive claims and abetted its confinement to a private realm. As Ian Barbour has argued, "We cannot remain content with a plurality of unrelated languages if they are languages about the same world. If we seek a coherent interpretation of all experience, we cannot avoid the search for a unified worldview."[7]

In many ways the closed, mechanistic worldview of Newtonian science forced the isolationist strategy of liberal theology. Twentieth century developments in science, especially, have begun to offer a very different conception of nature. Far from being construed as closed and static, nature increasingly appears as an open, dynamic process more akin to an integrated organism than to a machine. This fundamental revisioning of the natural order now makes possible a much needed reapprochement between religion and science.[8] Although it does not make room for what Charles Hartshorne called the monarchical ruler of classical theism, it does allow for an understanding of God and God's relationship to the created order that has deep biblical roots. The world of order and disorder to which modern physics has pointed is, in the words of John Polkinghorne, "a world kept in being by the divine juggler rather than by the divine Structural Engineer, a world whose precarious process speaks of the free gift of Love."[9]

Although the emphasis upon the complex combination of chance and law, openness and structure, freedom and determinancy, in the conception of the creative process once again makes room for God's continuing creativity, it clearly alters the traditional portrait of God's providential role in the cosmos. Beyond displacing humans from the center of the cosmic drama, the emerging picture of God's continuing creativity makes it difficult to construe God as the "divine protector" who is concerned for "each hair on our head." While this may be experienced as sheer loss, it does free us from the increasingly difficult task of reconciling this belief with our experiences in the world. Too many events befall us, both individually and collectively, that radically undermine this image of God. Moreover, efforts to sustain this traditional portrait of God in "his" fatherly love for humans appear not just heroic but obscene against the backdrop of the atrocities of the twentieth century. This is not to suggest that events prior to our own time did not strain this theological picture. One need only consider the fascination with the Book of Job and the exegetical efforts to mine this text throughout the past two millennia. But the collective weight and dominance of the traditional theological vision withstood the strain. In my judgment, it no longer can, and, just as importantly, it no longer should. The "underside" of the traditional emphasis upon God's primary relationship to humanity has become all too visible as have the tensions between a providential God and suffering and evil. For both moral and intellectual reasons, it behooves us to correct this distortion in our religious visions.

God's sustaining role, reflected in the divine ordering of cosmic life, becomes most visible in and through the consequences that follow from ignoring it. The failure of self and society to align themselves with the divine ordering is in traditional religious discourse the product and occasion of sin. Sin is not simply a private transgression between the self and God that can be righted by a personal confession. Such a spiritual construal of sin fails to recognize the very real consequences of sin for personal, social, and natural life. The flourishing and, indeed, very survival of life forms are threatened by the consequences of sin. The ecological crisis offers a vivid illustration of the material repercussions that follow from a failure to respect the divine ordering within cosmic life. Our inattention and indifference to the effects of our industrialization upon the ecosystem are only beginning

to emerge. But we can see that these effects have contributed
to the extinction of some life forms and to the diminished well-
being of many others, including our own. Our actions have
wrecked havoc upon the proper ordering of the network of
being within which we exist. We are now reaping the consequences, and slowly beginning to recognize that there is an
order to the ecosystem that we ignore only at great peril.

The consequences of such transgressions against the
divine ordering have in traditional religious discourse been
interpreted as the judgment and wrath of God. There is a
certain inexorability about this experience. Divine judgment
and wrath cannot be extirpated through personal prayer and
ritual.[10] Atonement consists of a continual process of rectifying
for prior transgressions by the self and by others, thereby
bringing personal and social life into greater conformity with
God's sustaining activity.[11] The divine ordering, in other
words, is real; transgressions against this order bring real
consequences, which are themselves often the clearest signs
of the underlying order.

To affirm God's role in ordering and shaping the cosmic
process does not mean that we can easily and unambiguously
identify the details of this role. To claim we could, of course,
presumptuously suggests that we have clear and direct access
to the will of God. On the other hand, neither is total
skepticism about God's ordering role appropriate. This
extreme, even when motivated by radical humility, does not
encourage the effort to discern God's activity within the
natural and human orders. It provides no compass by which
to guide our own responses. We are left between these two
poles, having to decipher the cosmic record in light of current
perceptions about what contributes to the survival and
flourishing of the interconnected network of being. Such
perceptions must be subject to continual revision as our
knowledge, including scientific and moral knowledge,
increases.

For the purposes of developing a public theology, the
significance of God's creative and sustaining roles in cosmic
life is a function of their ability to underscore the interconnectedness and value of the created order.

In this way monotheism provides powerful support for envisioning the public realm as a radically inclusive common life, a fundamentally interconnected matrix within which the actions of each reverberate for good or ill upon the whole. This interpretation of God calls into question theologies that domesticate God by aligning the divine purposes or interests to a subset of the whole. However ambiguous the cosmic record may be regarding the divine agency, it precludes making the individual, the nation, or even humanity the primary arena within which the divine life is operative. The great value in reemphasizing the creative and sustaining roles of God in our own time lies in their power to modify the modern, liberal trajectory that has made not just the human sphere, but often the individual, the locus of divine activity. Through reattention to God's creative and sustaining roles in cosmic life the self-aggrandizement of this trajectory is starkly revealed. Monotheism's inclusive thrust which simultaneously establishes intricate links within the whole can only rest with a vision of public life that is thoroughly interconnected in its form and radically universal in its scope.

However, the substantive task of a public theology is not adequately met through these emphases alone. Despite the importance of these motifs for expressing and legitimating a common life, they do not adequately depict the critical and transformative moments that must accompany its emergence. In other words, although they can play an important role in underscoring the reality of the interconnected network of being, these motifs run the danger of legitimating what is presently the case. The symbol of God the creator runs the risk of suggesting that the community of being is fully given as a consequence of creation's dependence upon the divine source. If we regard creation from the perspective of the divine creative source, the unity and value of what is would, in this theological scenario, be visible. Attention to the sustaining activity of God minimizes this tendency by locating the creative activity within an ongoing cosmic process; this move calls our attention to the direction of the cosmic process, suggesting that the divine intentions are not discernible through the fact of existence alone but in terms of the

God and Public Life   111

development and direction within creation. This is an
important step toward avoiding a divine sanctioning of the
status quo. But it does not go far enough. It remains too easy
to interpret God's sustaining role in terms of the order of
creation, rather than in terms of the ordering of creation. The
former traditional emphasis upon order lends itself to a
legitimation of the *current* order as it is manifested in the
natural, social, and political spheres. From this perspective
any behavior that undermines the given order is contrary to
the divine will. This is a dangerously conservative theological
justification of the status quo, which has throughout Western
history provided a divine sanction to the entrenched authorities. To avoid this kind of "sacred canopy," it is necessary
to emphasize a third motif: the redeeming activity of God.
Only in and through an exploration of the divine transformation of life can we begin to glimpse the ideal that stands
in judgment upon the current ordering of creation. For the
task of a public theology, the redeeming activity of God
provides the means for recognizing the deficiencies and
limitations in the common life as it currently exists. It
provides the rationale and the motivation for the extension
and critical transformation of our common life.

God as Redeemer

An emphasis upon God's redemptive role calls attention
to the fact that creation stands under divine judgment, that
it does not yet embody the fulfillment of the divine intentions.
It is this motif, then, that provides motivation and direction
to the perennial struggle to reform this life in light of the
eschatological goal toward which creation, it may be hoped,
asymptotically moves.

Although Christianity has always recognized God's
redemptive role, it has been subject to quite varied interpretations. One of the earliest and most enduring Christian
interpretations of redemption has centered upon the substi-
tutionary atonement of Jesus Christ. In this theological
scenario, redemption is associated with the appeasement of

a wrathful God. In place of the older Hebraic practice of animal sacrifices, Christians posited the once and for all sacrifice of Jesus Christ. Individual salvation, from this perspective, consists of the personal acceptance of God's saving actions in Jesus Christ. Much modern Christian theology has taken exception to this traditional view of redemption, contending that it is a mythological, even magical, view that has little connection with the real world. In line with the modern rejection of "otherworldly" realities, recent theologies have sought to interpret redemption in terms of the forces within this world that contribute to its salvation. Most vocal within this movement have been liberation theologians who insist upon connecting redemption with the overcoming of the actual conditions of oppression that mark the created order.

This rejection of an exclusively otherworldly or spiritual construal of salvation is also integral to the construction of a public theology. Unless God's redemptive actions are found within this world, the transformation of our common life receives little theological support. Indeed, as many have argued, otherworldly redemption tends to legitimate the oppressive conditions of this world by denying them ultimate status. Suffering will be compensated, injustices will be rectified, at some future time, in some other place. Although this view has clearly enabled its holders to cope with suffering and injustices, it has typically provided insufficient impetus for the transformation of current ills.

In order to underscore the critical moment in the extension and transformation of our common life, it is necessary to emphasize the redemptive activity of God within the historical arena. In this vein, I would suggest that God's redemptive role be considered in terms of the forces working to extend, deepen, and transform our common life into the universal community of being. The universal community, clearly, consists of more than simple interconnectedness; it consists of the interconnected network of being in which the ability of each to fulfill and enjoy its life potentialities is maximized. In this way a common life is transformed into a more genuine communal life which, so far as possible, sustains the well-being and flourishing of each member.

What such redemptive divine activity might mean within the natural order remains very enigmatic. Perhaps no more can be said at this point than the positing of some impulse toward increased complexity and consciousness within cosmic evolution. This claim in itself is relatively bold, and certainly subject to future disconfirmation. We are not limited to such a minimal delineation of God's redemptive role within the human arena however. For we are better positioned to identify the actions and conditions that are needed to extend and transform our common life into a genuine universal community.

Even as we engage in this task of specifying God's redemptive role, however, we must be aware of the risks, however unavoidable they may be. It is a task that is, at once, both necessary and dangerous. Identifying specific actions with God's redemptive role risks cloaking them with a divine legitimation they may not warrant. On the other hand, assiduously avoiding such a risk guarantees an unacceptably high level of theological abstraction. The former danger of sacralizing profane events has long been acknowledged, if not avoided, within the tradition. The dangers that attend too great a degree of theological generality, however, have only recently been recognized.

We are indebted to recent liberation theologies for exposing the dangers of theological abstractionism. Speaking of divine love, for instance, without attending to what such love means in specific historical contexts is, at one level, empty rhetoric. At a more serious level, however, such rhetoric, however inadvertently, tends to reinforce the status quo. The underlying assumption is that the universality of God's love precludes its identification with any particular cause or action. As liberation theologians have persuasively argued, such "divine impartiality" does not constitute impartiality within human conflicts. On the contrary, it constitutes a clear and unmistakable justification for the existing power relations within any situation. The refusal to identify any cause or struggle with God's redemptive role, however noble the motivation, functions to legitimate the current power alignments. Hence the suspicion within liberation theologies of utopian references that do not include more specific strategies for their realization. To avoid allowing theological abstractions to justify the current order, liberation theologies have insisted upon more specific identifications of divine intentions and activities. They have uncovered current forms of domination, including racism, poverty, and sexism, and insisted that God is present in the struggle to overcome such evils. In this way they provide religious legitimation to the struggle for social justice, and avoid the tacit endorsement of the reigning order of much traditional theological discourse.

A public theology needs to incorporate the critical edge that liberation theologies wield if it is to succeed in its agenda to reconstitute the public realm. Unless God's redemptive role is not only affirmed, but concretely identified, the holistic moment will obscure the distortions that characterize our common life. The result would be a theology that legitimated unity at the expense of justice, a common life at the expense of a communal life. To avoid this a public theology will need to look closely at the current social order, seeking to discern the attitudes, assumptions, and practices that undermine the mutuality and integrity of our common life and prevent its transformation into the universal community of being. For God's redemptive role will be linked with the actions directed toward removing the obstacles to genuine community.

The refusal to traffic in vague utopian references that are both atemporal and acontextual leads liberation theologians to identify God with particular struggles within society. In the earlier, and now classic, works of liberation theology, especially, God's liberating activity was largely limited to one such struggle. Thus in James Cone's *God of the Oppressed*, Gustavo Gutierrez's *The Theology of Liberation*, or Mary Daly's *Beyond God the Father*, for instance, God was interpreted in terms of the movement to end, respectively, racism, poverty, or sexism. An important development within liberation theology has been the gradual recognition of the legitimacy of other struggles and the correlative acknowledgement that oppression is typically multifaceted, not reducible to a single cause. As a result, God's redemptive role has been similarly expanded.

This enlargement of God's redemptive role is important for several distinct though related reasons. First, it corrects an excessively Manichaean strain in liberation theologies, reflected in their tendency to legitimate "us against them" outlooks. Dichotomizing the world in this fashion makes it much too easy to avoid self-criticism, much too easy to see "the other" as the locus of sin and moral culpability. As H. Richard Niebuhr more eloquently put it, in relationship to another form of Christian sectarianism, "the line between church and world runs through every soul, not between souls."[12] The need for reformation on the part of one's self and one's community is perennial this side of the eschaton. For this reason God's redemptive activity should not be narrowly linked with any single cause despite the rhetorical and political efficacy it may yield.

Expanding the scope of the work of divine transformation curbs the extreme preoccupation within liberation theologies upon structural evils and political and social activities. The initial turn to consider sin from a social or structural perspective has been an extremely important corrective to the prevailing tendency to construe sin in purely personal terms. However, it is no more adequate to link God's transforming work with large social causes to the exclusion of individual metanoia than to do the reverse.

In the process of moving beyond theological generalities we must avoid the trap of radically reducing the scope of God's redemptive actions. The divine role in the creation of the universal community is not a single thread, attributable to a being, but multiple threads woven together from the whole fabric of being. The model of God that this presupposes is not a single being standing over against the whole of being, but a characterization of the nature of and potentiality within being itself. God and humanity within this theological framework do not stand in opposition. Humans, rather, participate in the divine life. We are its embodiment, not alone but with other forms of life. Each, to very differing degrees, either contributes to or thwarts the creation of the universal community of being. Moving beyond a reified, oppositionally construed interpretation of God is critical to overcoming the imperialistic, patriarchal propensities of monotheism.[13]

My interpretation of God's redemptive role is noticeably silent about the theological significance of Jesus. My silence is in part deliberate insofar as a public theology is most dependent, as I noted earlier, upon an adequate interpretation of God. Moreover, the Christocentric focus of much American Christianity is symptomatic of the very individualistic, anthropocentric worldview that a public theology seeks to combat. Nonetheless there is certainly a place for a reformulated Christology within a Christian public theology. Indeed the symbol of the incarnation can serve as a powerful tool for overcoming the traditional dualism between God and the world that has contributed to the devaluation of the body, nature, and women. Incarnational symbolism, combined with an emphasis upon the coming of the Spirit, can be appropriated to underscore the intimate connection between the divine and the comos. Far from perpetuating the dualism between God and the world which ushers in the alienation of humanity from nature, this symbolism can serve to radically affirm humanity and the wider natural matrix within which it is embedded by construing them as embodiments of the divine life.[14] Developing such a Christology, although beyond the scope of this study, would be a natural extension of the project to develop a public theology.

Concluding Observations

Developing an interpretation of God through the classical roles of creator, sustainer, and redeemer is designed to illuminate the substantive affinity between monotheism, properly interpreted, and the proposed reconfiguration of public life. The point is that devotion to God is not compatible either with a retreat from the public realm or, as importantly, with indifference as to its configuration. As we have seen, however, the appropriate envisioning of public life depends upon the reaffirmation of religious strands largely submerged within the modern ethos.

Critical for the development of a public theology is an interpretation of God that facilitates two moments: the holistic moment and the critical moment. The holistic moment generates a respectful sense of the whole, a recognition of the interconnectedness and value of the created order. It constitutes the recognition of a fundamental commonality that unites all being. But this insight, far from functioning as a self-contained intuition, should provide the ground and motivation for the critical moment which fixates upon the disparity between the present order of creation and a redeemed common life, the eschatological community of being. An interpretation of God, then, must strive to keep these moments in a creative dialectical tension. The perennial danger is that an interpretation of God will fail in this dialectical task, generating one moment to the exclusion of the other.

Too strong or exclusive an accent upon the holistic moment turns monotheism into a powerful legitimation of the current orders of creation. It fixates upon a spiritual oneness that turns, whether contentedly or resignedly in upon itself, rather than outward which makes possible the sense of disjunction between this religious intuition and the world as unredeemed. This disjunction, interpreted in terms of judgment, issues forth the prescription to remake the world in the divine image. As Rachel Adler has put it, "the obligation to do justice is derived relationally, and rests upon a prerequisite obligation to perceive a likeness to self in the other."[15] The ground of justice, however, must not be confused with the exercise of justice. "Justice is the reshaping of our actions and institutions to express this sense of commonality in our everyday life."[16] Without the prior recognition of commonality, however, the rationale and motivation to pursue justice is displaced. The symbolism of God, in at least one of its trajectories, has the ontological and normative implications to foster the creative dialectical tension between the holistic and critical moments. Extending this trajectory, then, constitutes the indispensable substantive task of a public theology.

To reiterate, the agenda underlying this abbreviated theological sketch is to underscore the substantive affinity between the proposed reconfiguration of public life and monotheism, properly interpreted. This affinity is critical to the larger project to create a public theology. As we have seen in the preceding chapter, the reigning interpretation of public life receives support and legitimation from the tradition of classical liberalism which, I have suggested, has crystallized into a powerful contemporary myth. My interest is not in dismantling this myth—probably impossible given its role in American life and imagination and certainly unwise given its historic ability to enhance the freedom and rights of the individual—but in revising it. Theology can play an important, perhaps indispensable, role in this process of mythic revisioning. For monotheism, interpreted along the lines sketched above, possesses a unique ability to elicit recognition of and commitment to a radically inclusive common life that stands under judgment of a redemptive ideal demanding a perennial moral struggle for its attainment. Taken in this sense monotheism is less the pragmatic corollary of the proposed reconfiguration of public life than the cosmological-moral horizon that has made possible this revisioning of public life.

Chapter Five

Theology and Professional Boundaries

Any depiction of the nature of public theology must at some point confront questions concerning the appropriate style and audience for this kind of writing. All too often such issues are either ignored or relegated to a very secondary status, peripheral to what are taken to be the central matters of substance and method. Indeed there are forces within twentieth century intellectual life and its primary institutional matrix, the modern research university, that conspire to veil the importance of what are generally considered "rhetorical" or, more aptly, "merely rhetorical" issues. Even though contemporary academe may downplay the significance of audience and style in its exploration of texts and discourse, something about the word "public" pulls us toward a consideration of these issues.

Public discourse is typically regarded as that which is generally available, that is, not limited to a few. We have already considered an aspect of this issue in and through the contrast between public and parochial. In that context I argued that we needed to make a distinction between parochial and contextual reflection in order to move beyond an ahistorical interpretation of rationality that equates public with universal intelligibility. Escaping from this impossible expectation makes clear that contextually rooted reflection does not preclude its public status. It is important to recognize, however, that parochialism is not the only obstacle to public discourse. It is also possible for reflection to be so professionalized that it is effectively precluded from public consumption. Instead of being intelligible to the general educated public, it is written by and for a select few who have been initiated into a small professional guild. From this angle it is not the contrast between public and parochial with which we are dealing, but that between public and professional.

The primary reference to the term "profession," of course, is to forms of occupation that share salient characteristics, with law and medicine serving as primary paradigms. Although scholars differ over precisely which occupational characteristics apply, the most frequently cited criteria include extensive training with a significant intellectual component, culminating in an advanced degree and the provision of an important service to society.[1] Because the rise of professionalism was a process not an event, it is difficult to date its emergence without slighting antecedent roots. In its modern form, however, professionalization is regarded as a fairly recent phenomenon, for the most part a product of the middle to late nineteenth century. While useful in locating a reference for "profession," the occupational criteria cited above do not capture the intricate web of assumptions, values, and effects associated with the rise of professionalism in modern society. So pervasive has been its influence in defining the identity and goals of the American middle class, it has in effect forged a "culture of professionalism."[2]

The modern research university has been the primary institutional vehicle for this emerging professional culture. Its organizational divisions and standards reflect and reinforce the assumptions and values of the professional culture that it inhabits. Modern academic theology inevitably absorbs and refracts the influences from this institutional setting. Thus the professionalization of the wider culture as well as the more specific institutional pressures of the modern university have combined to produce a form of professional academic theology that is largely unavailable to the general educated public. Theological writing within the academy has increasingly become a form of technical discourse that is only understood by colleagues with similar professional training. With the rise of secularization and subsequent displacement of religion from the center of intellectual and social life, the professional trajectory has contributed to the marginalization of theology, as theologians speak to theologians who speak to theologians. . . .The question, of course, is: to what end?

This chapter is primarily devoted to telling this story. By filling in some of the details of the "culture of professionalism" and its institutional vehicle, the modern research university, the forces that have contributed to the formation and perpetuation of a professionalized theology will become more visible. In large part my aim is to bring professionalization into the foreground, in the subversive attempt to make its all too customary presence appear more problematic.

But the project to create a more public theology means that diagnostic efforts alone, however necessary, are insufficient. What, if anything, can be done to counteract the trend toward professionalization that has insulated and isolated theologians from a wider public? There are no easy answers. This observation is hardly surprising, of course, given the complex forces that have contributed to the current situation. Even so, I do want to chart a direction that may help, eventually, to minimize the professional ghettoization into which theology has fallen. To anticipate, I shall argue that it is not enough for theologians to strive to speak intelligibly to nonacademics, however important and difficult that effort alone may be. Equally necessary, in my judgment, is a redrawing of the professional boundaries that over the centuries have come to demarcate theological reflection. The genre of theology as it has traditionally been practiced is itself, now, part of the problem. Theologians must help to reorient the genre, away from the dominant focus upon the text and toward a more thorough and sustained engagement with religious beliefs and practices as they are embodied in particular cultural contexts. This remedy to the problem of professionalization stands in marked contrast to the remedy that has commanded the widest appeal in recent years—the genre of narrative theology. Although the increasingly popular strategy of narrative theology does enlarge the theological audience by including laity, it is not, I shall argue, the most appropriate model of a public theology.

Our primary focus will be on some of the features and repercussions of twentieth century professionalization, particularly as they have effected the doing of theology. But first a retrospective glance at theology and professionalization is in order to provide some perspective on the current situation. Because the overriding agenda in this work is constructive rather than historical, no comprehensive review will be attempted.[3]

A Retrospective Glance

The professionalization of earlier forms of theology varied significantly, depending not only upon the time but, as importantly, upon the institutional location of the theologian. In very general terms, one can trace growing professionalization within the genre as biblical commentary rooted within the monastic tradition was displaced by the rise of dialectic, speculative theology within the medieval university. Luther and the reformers constitute, in many respects, a deliberate rejection of the tradition of medieval scholastic theology, greatly motivated by the desire to gain a wide audience for their reform movement. Despite its immediate success, Luther's solution to the problem of professionalization is not, I shall argue, a viable option for a contemporary public theology.

Christian theology throughout its first millennia was largely biblical commentary closely connected to the devotional life of the writer and his or her community. The Bible was not simply the authoritative text that adjudicated between various theological alternatives. It was more like the central source or wellspring that nourished, structured, and controlled theological reflection. Christian theology was also closely aligned with the proper interior stance of the writer. Sound biblical commentary was assumed to depend upon the illumination of the mind by the Holy Spirit. In this theological genre prose was frequently interspersed with petitions and prayers seeking divine guidance and offering praise and thanksgiving. The characteristic location of theology within the monasteries into the middle ages helped to ensure this concern with the devotional life of the theologian. Theology was considered a form of wisdom made possible by the guidance of the Spirit as one contemplated through discipline and prayer the revelatory deposits of the tradition, especially the biblical text. The appropriation of classical learning, as Augustine certainly recognized, threatened the communal value of theology insofar as it effectively narrowed the audience to the highly educated. To counteract this tendency, Augustine, for instance, delineated a "Christian learning" that could meet the needs of a wider community. Indeed "this deliberate subordination of the scholarly and technical to the needs of the general reader continued within the monastic tradition into the medieval period."[4]

The development of theology into an academic discipline was a slow process, occurring in tandem with the transformation of the monastic and cathedral schools into the medieval universities in the late twelfth and thirteenth centuries. The rise of the universities contributed to the emergence of a new theological paradigm as theology was transformed into a systematic, speculative enterprise more at home in the classroom than the monastery. The professionalizing forces that had been held in check by theology's deep spiritual and biblical roots gained momentum, eventuating in a new theological genre with its own distinctive style.

Rather than limiting themselves to biblical commentary, theologians increasingly engaged in dialectics, a form of reasoning that explored problems, inconsistencies, and alternatives in a logical fashion. Great effort was made to achieve a rational, systematic order for theological reflection, an order based on conceptual organization rather than on the chronology of the Scriptures. Scholastic theology in the late middle ages more and more assumed the form of technical, scholarly discourse that was divorced from the devotional and practical life of the individual and congregation. A common discourse based on biblical images, symbols, and narratives was increasingly displaced by specialized terminology that few had mastered. There is some indication that the academization of theology in the twelfth and thirteenth centuries contributed to the emergence in the late middle ages of a genre of mystical writing that was, as a reactive strategy, firmly rooted in personal religious experience.[5]

Luther and the reformers also represent a reaction to scholastic, academic theology of the late middle ages, although a reaction that was more indebted to humanism and the Renaissance than to the mystical tradition and its earlier antecedents in monastic theology. Regarding the period from the early Christian era to his own time as an aberration in Christianity, Luther urged a return to the Bible and its earliest interpreters. He scorned scholastic theology with its technical preoccupations and language that rendered it beyond the comprehension of the general population. His genuine interest in addressing the religious needs of the laity and in fostering a successful revitalization movement within Christianity compelled him to develop theological strategies and styles that would make possible communication to a general audience. Hence he returned to the use of a shared biblical discourse that was intelligible to nonexperts. Just as importantly, he opted to write in the vernacular rather than Latin which had been the prevailing language of learned culture of European civilization.[6] With this decision, inseparable from his recognition of the opportunities that the new technology of the printing press afforded in mass communication, Luther was extraordinarily successful in expanding the scope of his audience.[7]

There is no disputing the fact that contemporary academic theology, in terms of professional characteristics, stands closer to medieval scholastic theology than to the far more widely circulated theological writings of Luther and the reformers or to the earlier monastic theological tradition. The split between learned culture and lay culture is in our own day not unlike that of the medieval period. The causes for this split, however, have changed considerably. The linguistic gap between the two cultures has ended, as has the general nonliteracy of the population and the prohibitive cost and scarcity of books. Other forces, however, associated with the emergence of a "culture of professionalism" have arisen to perpetuate, indeed exacerbate, the professional isolation and marginalization of theology. Before considering how contemporary theologians might lessen the professional ghettoization of their field, it is necessary to consider the current dynamics sustaining this isolation.

The Professionalization of American Culture

Multiple factors coalesced in mid-nineteenth century America to produce the push toward professionalization. The most important factor was the increasing complexity of modern life, related especially to urbanization and rapidly advancing technologies that created a significant demand for highly trained specialists. The professional met this demand by mastering a body of systematic knowledge, securing social accreditation, and contributing his or her expertise to the benefit of society as a whole. It is certainly beyond the parameters of this study to provide a detailed analysis of the causes, characteristics, and effects of the professionalization of modern life. For our purposes two facets of this development are particularly relevant. The first consists in the emergence of the modern university which assumed its present shape under the influence of the professionalizing forces that were transforming the culture as a whole. More than any other institution, its ethos and structure have reflected and furthered the professional evolution of society. Our second angle on the rise of professionalization is broader in scope, attending to the cultural diffusion of the professional ethos within the wider society. This perspective, which considers professionalism in relationship to issues of identity, status, and power, illuminates the deeply rooted attitudes that contribute to the maintenance of our professionalized world.

Specialization and the Modern University

The modern university was the institution that provided the training and accreditation that were needed to meet the growing demand for specialists in an increasingly complex, technological society. Rapid social changes contributed to a great explosion of and specialization in various fields of inquiry, producing major transformations in the university and its curriculum. The areas of classical study splintered into discrete disciplines as new methods and tools were crafted for purposes of research. Psychology, for instance, was carved out of its former home in philosophy in the first decades of the twentieth century and sociology emerged as an autonomous discipline during this period as well. Whereas professors formerly received a broad classical education, and could teach across a spectrum of subject areas, they increasingly were trained in a particular specialized discipline that comprised the boundaries for their teaching and research. In 1870 American institutions awarded only one doctorate; in 1884, little more than one hundred years ago, only 10 percent of the Harvard faculty held the doctorate.[8] These figures changed dramatically within a few decades as the forces of professionalization swept through the university.

The professionalization of higher education with its attendant push toward specialization created an increasing gap between the university and the wider culture. Bruce Kuklick has traced this development within American philosophy. The commitment to communicate to a general public and apply expertise to social problems that characterized nineteenth century philosophers evaporated as professionalism and the specialization it spawned gained ascendency. As Kuklick explains, after World War I "the order of the day was technical specialized research published for technically competent audiences in technical journals, with popularizations in all areas of speculation frequently relegated to hacks, incompetents, and has-beens."[9] Specialization that had formerly been pursued for its eventual application to general problems of life outside the university increasingly became an end in itself.

Socialization into professional, specialized academic life in the twentieth century has been highly successful. Kuklick's description of specialized research remains a succinct depiction of "serious scholarship." It appears quite natural and appropriate within the reigning academic ethos, and it is continually reinforced by the procedures and policies surrounding tenure and promotion decisions. Describing the mutual reinforcement of institutional procedures and the reigning academic ethos, Edward Farley writes:

> The kind of research and scholarship the tenure time clock promotes is very much that which the specialism of the graduate school has already anticipated: specialty research.

Accordingly, the young scholar either continues the dissertation specialty or quickly locates a new and equally narrow specialty. Once tenure is obtained, the scholar-teacher continues to build up a corpus of specialty studies in order to achieve promotion to full professor. Thus, the reward system encourages the scholar-teacher to begin in and remain in a specialty field; it affords little or no chance to explore broader territories, alternate paradigms, or the contours of the discipline itself.[10]

Not only does this paradigm of scholarship enlarge the gap between the university and the culture at large, but it contributes to the devaluation of teaching. Students, after all, are not professional colleagues but members of the "general public" who infiltrate the insulated research academy for brief stays. The very high esteem in which specialized research is held, then, itself contributes to the depreciation of teaching which, far from advancing the frontiers of scholarship, requires the university professor to make connections between scholarship and the culture at large.

It is certainly not my intent to deny that much good has come from these developments. Our knowledge across space and time has increased immeasurably as a result of these transformations. On the other hand, it is also important to recognize that the benefits have not been without their costs. There has been an increasing sense that the pendulum has swung too far. The clear and distinct gains secured by specialization have been offset not only by the loss of a much needed generalist perspective but by the isolation of the academy from the wider culture. This is especially problematic within the humanities. The important insights and technical applications that come from specialized studies within the sciences are all too often not forthcoming from comparable specialization within the humanities. Consider, for instance, Cornel West's criticisms of the professional boundaries operative in the discipline of philosophy:

The professional discipline of philosophy is presently caught in an interregnum; mindful of the dead ends of analytical modes of philosophizing, it is yet unwilling to move into the frightening wilderness of pragmatism and historicism with their concomitant concerns in social theory, cultural criticism, and historiography. This situation has left the discipline with an excess of academic rigor yet bereft of substantive intellectual vigor and uncertain of a legitimate subject matter. The unwillingness of many philosophers to tread in the wilderness results from adherence to professional boundaries and academic self-understandings. To put it crudely, most philosophers are neither trained to converse with literary critics, historians, and social theorists nor ready to give up the secure self-image of academicians engaged in "serious" philosophical research.[11]

To understand how deeply rooted is the problem, it is necessary to consider the intersections of power, status, and identity in American society. Understanding these connections makes clear that the reconfiguration of professional boundaries is far from simply an academic issue.

The Ideology of Professionalism

The emergence of the modern university during the latter half of the nineteenth century reflected and furthered the development of an ideology of professionalism which became the prevailing worldview and ethos of the middle class, generating the identity, values, and goals for the majority of Americans. For more than a century the professional has commanded high social status within American society. The point is, of course, unsurprising: high intellectual achievement combined with a clear service ideal has elicited a broadly based respect. But the attraction, then and now, runs deeper. Consider the larger context within which the professional emerged. The Enlightenment vision, captured in the cry for "liberté, fraternité, and egalité," contributed to the erosion of the traditional ecclesiastical, political, and social authorities. Into this ideological vacuum of legitimate power stepped the professional whose claim to authority rested solely upon science. To invoke science was to invoke that which was objectively true—there, in principle, for all to see, although, in actuality, only visible to those few who were adequately trained. The professional, then, through the legitimation of science, assumed the role of authority, the expert, to be trusted, respected, and heeded by society as a whole. To withhold one's respect and compliance was tantamount to rejecting science—that is, to be irrational. As Bledstein succinctly puts it, "Professions controlled the magic circle of scientific knowledge which only the few, specialized by training and indoctrination, were privileged to enter, but which all in the name of nature's universality were obligated to appreciate."[12]

The attractions of the professional life were many, especially for members of the middle class who had not only the desire but the opportunity to distinguish themselves. It was a way to achieve status and power without compromising the prevailing democratic, egalitarian ideology. Moreover, it did so without sacrificing the freedom and autonomy of the individual. After the requisite training and certification, professionals were largely exempt from external control or judgment, excepting, of course, the self-legislation of the professional group itself. Here, again, the professional epitomized the very traits that the Enlightenment ethos valued most highly. From this perspective, it is easy to understand the rapid spread of professional aspirations within the American middle class. No longer were professionals limited to law, ministry, and medicine. Members from a wide range of occupations clamored for professional status. In the latter half of the nineteenth century, teachers, social workers, funeral directors, even plumbers, aspired to the ranks of the professionals.

The rapid spread of professional associations across a broad spectrum of occupations was a reflection of a much deeper transformation occurring in American culture. For the rise of professionalism signaled more than the organization and standardization of various forms of work. At a more basic level it constituted a change in the formation of personal identity, including the values and goals that it generated. Increasingly individual identity became a function of professional affiliation and success. The local associations which, traditionally, had provided the context for identity weakened as career, advancement, and the material success that accompanied it emerged as the primary foci of self-definition. As Bledstein writes, ". . . Americans began to identify themselves in terms not used by their fathers: by individual advancement in a career and by the degree of passion for the material symbols of success rather than by social rank, region, and community obligation."[13] The corporate dimensions that had defined an individual life weakened as an individualistic, "vertical" model for identity gained ascendency. Vertical mobility, getting ahead in one's career, emerged as a central preoccupation and goal. Although this was most evident in the developing professions, the ethos became a defining characteristic of the middle class as a whole.[14]

The role of professionalism in the formation of identity intensified its effects. The meaning and value that accrued from a successful professional life went beyond simple occupational achievement. Consequently, the need to attain and secure professional affiliation was felt even more deeply. Bruce Wilshire in his recent study *The Moral Collapse of the University* persuasively argues that the modern thrust for professional identity has generated powerful "archaic initiational and purificational practices which establish the identity of group and individual member through the exclusion of the unwashed and uncertified. . . ."[15] Elaborate rituals and taboos have evolved that both reflect and sustain the gap between the professional "initiate" and the outsider who is radically "other"—ignorant, helpless, even pitiable. Professional identity, then, is sustained through multifarious attitudes and behaviors that maintain a strict opposition between the initiated member and outsiders. Deliberate or inadvertent moves to bridge the gap are experienced as radically polluting. For the failure to maintain a clear separation between the two constitutes a direct challenge to the oppositionally defined professional identity.

At this point we need to turn our attention from diagnostic forays into the history and ethos of professionalism to the constructive agenda that guides this work. What strategies should theologians adopt to counteract the isolation that has resulted from rigid professional boundaries? Unless some headway can be made in this direction, the possibility of a genuinely public theology appears very remote.

Redrawing the Boundaries of Theology: A Bilateral Offensive

Recognizing the ideology of professionalism that shapes identity, power, and status in American society makes exceedingly clear the obstacles that block efforts to create a more public theology. The most obvious barrier is that which separates the academician from the general public. Writing which intends to communicate to a wider audience weakens the barrier, thereby threatening the distinctive purity, and hence perceived expertise, of the professional camp. One suspects this must be especially threatening to theologians whose expertise has already been severely challenged by the rise of a secular culture, especially the secular research university.

But professional boundaries do more than isolate the academician from a wider public. They reflect and reinforce the isolation of one disciplinary genre from another. Since professional identity is always a function of a particular field of expertise, the legitimacy and distinctiveness of the field must be preserved to sustain the identity.

A public theology is one that seeks to minimize the professional boundaries that isolate and insulate theology from a wider audience. It is important to keep in mind that the boundaries border two different fronts; there is the line separating theologians from a general audience as well as the one separating theologians from academicians in other disciplines. In the endeavor to develop a more public theology, it is especially important that both boundaries be reconfigured.

Indeed it is the failure to address both boundaries that seriously weakens the most widely heralded strategy to combat professionalization within theology. The genre of narrative theology has been touted in recent years as a way of expanding the theological audience. Reappropriating biblical symbolism and stories as the lens through which to interpret contemporary experience would, its defenders argue, not only ensure an authentically Christian theology but it would enable theologians to communicate to the faithful in an accessible, indeed engaging, style. Although I find this concern to broaden the audience very commendable, a biblical narrative theology strikes me as a sectarian strategy that is not appropriate for the development of a public theology. Although narrative theology does avoid the isolating trap of excessive professionalization, its very success on this front often comes by slighting other important dimensions in the notion of public.

Intratextual Biblical Theology: A Confessional Alternative

The most influential description and defense of a narrative biblical theology is found in George Lindbeck's *The Nature of Doctrine: Religion and Theology in a Postliberal Age.* Lindbeck roots his analysis and defense of an intratextual biblical theology in the postmodern insight into the historicity and multiplicity of the cultural worldviews that shape experience. Instead of lamenting the radical relativism that this insight might engender, Lindbeck uses it to underscore the historicity of human life and thought, the traditioned character of all human experience and reflection. Indeed the great strength of this form of theology, in my view, is precisely this emphasis upon the the role and importance of tradition in shaping individuals and cultures. However, the way Lindbeck interprets traditions and the status he accords them in theology are far more problematic.

Lindbeck is particularly interested in identifying what is discernibly Christian within the Christian tradition, given the enormous variation it has evidenced through the centuries. The unifying element within Christianity, Lindbeck suggests, cannot be found in constancy at the level of theological propositions, symbols, or experiences. These change according to place and time. The constancy is, he argues, grammatical in nature; it is a product of the biblical text through which Christians have sought to interpret the world beyond the text. Hence Lindbeck writes: "What is important is that Christians allow their cultural conditions and highly diverse affections to be molded by the set of biblical stories that stretches from creation to eschaton and culminates in Jesus' passion and resurrection."[16] The constancy of the biblical framework ensures the unity and authenticity of the tradition as it encounters radically diverse cultures. Thus Lindbeck concludes that "it is the religion instantiated in Scripture which defines being, truth, goodness, and beauty, and the nonscriptural exemplifications of these realities need to be transformed into figures (or types or antitypes) of the scriptural ones."[17]

The limitations in Lindbeck's intratextual biblical theology are a function of his interpretation of the nature and status of tradition. On a descriptive level, it is questionable that the coherence of traditions is a product of an underlying grammar rooted in a sacred constituting text. From this perspective a tradition is at its core static, with only a surface dynamism resulting from the interaction of this foundational grammar in varied contexts. This interpretation of a tradition is not only descriptively inadequate, in my judgment, but it incorporates a questionable evaluative preference for the originating elements of a tradition.

The descriptive inadequacy of this interpretation of a tradition stems from the questionable status accorded a grammar in Lindbeck's framework. Put simply, what is the justification for distinguishing within a complex dynamic tradition between an unchanging grammatical core and the diversity that purportedly results from the instantiation of the grammar in different settings? As Wayne Proudfoot has persuasively argued, Lindbeck's distinction between a grammar and a proposition about the world not only imputs a false constancy to a grammar but it rests upon too sharp a differentiation between a grammar and the first order propositions about the world that a grammar gives rise to: "Willard Quine, one of the most distinguished recent pragmatists, has shown that such a distinction is only relative, even in the linguistic case."[18] The motive behind Lindbeck's distinction, Proudfoot contends, is to secure for religion a logical status that renders it safe from the challenges of science and other first order propositions about the world.

Even beyond the descriptive adequacy of Lindbeck's interpretation of a tradition, however, is the question of its evaluative preference for its originating elements. A Lindbeckian construal of tradition generates a clear mandate to the theologian to return to the originating grammar rather than to engage the tradition as a whole in its varied complexity. From this perspective the tradition is not like a "chain novel" that the theologian seeks to extend. That model grants too much influence to the diverse elements within the tradition that have resulted from the diachronic interactions of the sacred text in different times and places. For Lindbeck the authenticity of the tradition is preserved when the theologian stands within the horizon of the biblical text, using it as the lens from which to interpret the world. But why privilege this text exclusively, why "assume that it defines being, truth, goodness, and beauty?"

Lindbeck's extremely important emphasis upon the role of tradition in shaping human life and thought is assimilated to a neo-Barthian proclamatory theology. Under the guise of a postmodern embrace of historicity, the concern shifts from what is true to what is authentically Christian, the latter becoming the controlling question as the former is consigned to the compost of modernity. The problems with this shift become most apparent in light of the diversity of traditions that constitute us. In an increasingly pluralist world does any one of us really inhabit a single tradition which can be, or should be, isolated from the multiple historical trajectories which shape us individually and collectively? As I consider my own situation, for example, it becomes clear that various historical streams intersect in my own identity pulling me in different directions. In the most general of terms I can recognize, for example, the traditions of modernity, America, Christianity, and feminism, refracted through a white, middle-class perspective, as fundamentally constitutive of who I am. Selecting one of these traditions (which themselves are highly complex) through which to interpret and evaluate the others only makes sense in light of prior assumptions regarding its truth. Such assumptions are not given with the transition to postmodernity. Rather than appropriating one of these traditions as the privileged lens through which to read and evaluate the others, it is necessary to struggle with the respective claims and insights of each.[19] Through this effort, individual identity is forged and traditions are extended, each the product of complex interactions which generate the unceasing effort to articulate more adequate and more coherent narratives for the self and for the society.

Lindbeck's intratextual biblical theology, in my judgment, prematurely abandons this unending struggle by selecting one tradition, or, rather, its originating, constituting text, as privileged from the start. For centuries this theological model was persuasive given the assumptions regarding the Bible as God's revelatory word. It is a theological model that cannot be sustained apart from these assumptions. This does not mean, of course, that theologians suddenly become indifferent to the Bible, as I explained in the defense of an extensionalist theology in chapter 2. If the theologian is seeking to extend the tradition, to create a coherent narrative that is worth telling now, the Bible will play a considerable role in determining appropriate fit. But it is not the only factor in determining fit, nor is strict continuity with the past the only criterion in interpretation. Hence for an extensionalist theology the Bible, while an important resource, is certainly not the lens through which extratextual realities are interpreted.

Those who advocate the genre of intratextual biblical theology as a device to expand the theological audience err in their exclusive concern with the boundary between the theologian and the laity. That is certainly one professional barrier that needs to be lowered. But it must not be reconfigured in isolation, less theology abandon its longstanding academic liaisons. Those who think that the world has clearly "gone to the devil" may well think this is the proper, prophetic alternative. If academia and the wider culture are utterly assimilated to "the world," then a sectarian theological model is inevitable. From such a perspective, a public theology is an oxymoron, and the proper institutional home for the theologian is the church.

This project to develop a public theology, of course, assumes otherwise. Hence it depends not just upon including more laity within the theological circle but in extending the interdisciplinary exchanges linking theology with other academic inquiries. It is easy enough to articulate such a goal. The more troubling questions, of course, remain: Is this goal even possible? If it is possible, how is it to be achieved?

Tracy's Three Publics: The Dangers of Fragmentation

Before addressing these questions, however, I would like to consider briefly David Tracy's contribution to the general issue of theology and its audience. Although he is not explicitly interested in the obstacles of professionalization, his analysis of the various "publics" or audiences that theology addresses is nonetheless relevant to the topic. As we have seen, for Tracy there is a public character to all theology that follows from the universal reality of God. However, because theology is addressed to varied social realities in the contemporary world, the form of publicness that it assumes will differ. Hence Tracy distinguishes between the three theological subdisciplines of fundamental, systematic, and practical theology that are primarily addressed, respectively, to the academy, the church, and society. Although Tracy insists that the subdisciplines are related and that the theologian implicitly addresses all three publics, the difference between the three forms of theology and the isolation of the three audiences is, as I read his work, far more pronounced. Although his typology is, in my judgment, a very useful device for sorting out the varied forms of contemporary theology, it is far more adequate as a description of contemporary theology than as a prescription for its future. His depiction of each theological type, far from justifying their continuation, suggests the need for moving toward their reintegration.

The three types of theology are differentiated, Tracy suggests, according to, among other things, audience, fundamental commitment, form of argumentation, and plausibility structure. Consider, for instance, the distinguishing features of fundamental theologies, systematic theologies, and practical theologies in terms of their form of argumentation. "Fundamental theologies will be concerned principally to provide arguments that all reasonable persons, whether 'religiously involved' or not, can recognize as reasonable."[20] Systematic theologies, on the other hand, "will have as their major concern the re-presentation, the reinterpretation of what is assumed to be the ever-present disclosive and trans-formative power of the particular religious tradition to which the theologian belongs."[21] And practical theologies "will ordinarily show less explicit concern with all theories and theoretical arguments. They will assume praxis as the proper criterion for the meaning and truth of theology...."[22] This difference in form of argumentation reflects different ethical stances as well.

> Fundamental theologies will be concerned principally with the ethical stance of honest, critical inquiry proper to its academic setting. Systematic theologies will be concerned principally with the ethical stance of loyalty or creative and critical fidelity to some classical religious tradition proper to its church relationship. Practical theologies will be concerned principally with the ethical stance of responsible commitment to and sometimes even involvement in a situation of praxis.[23]

Tracy's analysis is an extremely illuminating study of the varied types of theology that inhabit the contemporary scene. However, distinguishing them, and, more importantly, in claiming each reflects a genuine form of public argumentation addressed to a separate social reality, Tracy legitimates all three forms. As a consequence, the isolation of the three social realities, and their questionable assumptions regarding appropriate argumentation, are not challenged but reinforced.

We have already had occasion in an earlier chapter to consider the problems in holding that fundamental theology and systematic theology embody different, but analogous and equally legitimate, senses of public. In that context I argued that these two senses of public reflect incommensurate interpretations of rationality. In this chapter I am more interested in the way in which Tracy's discussion of the three subdisciplines of theology reinforces the isolation of the academy, the church, and the society, thereby legitimating the fracturing of theology into elements that should not stand alone.

Tracy repeatedly argues that these three modes of theology are analogous not separate. Nevertheless, the very sophistication and complexity of Tracy's portrait of each type leads, not toward a recognition of their purported underlying similarity, but to the endorsement of their isolated pursuit. The problem, then, is that open, honest inquiry, loyalty to a religious tradition, and commitment to praxis are too easily separated and allowed to operate in isolation from the others. What we need most, I would suggest, is not a way to justify these various pursuits but a way to bring them closer together. Their distinction reinforces the splits between reason and faith or theory and action or interpretation and application that have proved so problematic. As liberation theologians have argued so forcefully, theoretical reflection divorced from explicit commitments to praxis and advocacy is a misleading and dangerous modern ideology. By the same token, liberation theologies have themselves been strongly criticized for emphasizing liberation and witness to the exclusion of sufficient clarification and defense of their theoretical commitments.[24] These mutual criticisms reflect the distortions that attend theologies that are not sufficiently comprehensive in the social realities to which they respond.

The disciplinary distinctions, then, inadvertently reinforce the very tendencies that Tracy deplores in contemporary theology. Consider his powerful warning of the dangers that will come with a failure to address the complexity of the social reality of the theologian:

> For the results of that refusal lie all about us in the contemporary theological context: a relaxed if not lazy pluralism contenting itself with sharing private stories while both the authentically public character of every good story and the real needs of the wider society go unremarked; a passionate intensity masked as authentic prophecy that resists necessary pleas for empirical evidence while demanding compliance to a particular ideology; a

rush to the right for the false security of yet another restoration—too often a restoration which, like that of the Bourbons, has forgotten nothing and learned nothing; a reigning pathos among those who still demand argument and evidence (in a word, publicness) and whose inability to cut through the swamp of privateness may finally force them to become those who lack all conviction.[25]

These very penetrating criticisms of contemporary theology strike me as calling into question the disciplinary distinctions into which theology has fragmented. Tracy is absolutely right, I think, to insist that theology "face the complexity of the social reality of the theologian." But is this social reality adequately understood in terms of the three audiences that he identifies, with their respective modes of argumentation and interests? I would suggest that the very internalization of diverse social realities within the theologian renders those divisions problematic. As Tracy notes, the theologian is "an intellectual related to three publics, socialized in each, internalizing their sometimes divergent plausibility structures, in a symbiosis often so personal, complex and sometimes unconscious that conflicts on particular issues must be taken singly or 'retail,' not globally or wholesale."[26] If the theologian in our pluralistic world is thusly constituted in this complex way, then presumably so are many members of his or her audience. Should we continue to think in terms of distinctive social realities of church, academy, and society mandating profoundly different forms of theological reflection or should we make greater efforts to build bridges between these constituencies? If the latter, as I would argue, then we are most in need of a more integrated model of theology that, reflecting the internal struggle of the theologian to forge a persuasive synthesis, is responsive to all three publics in its attempt to be faithful to the universal God that underlies and unites them.

Building bridges between various constituencies, of course, is not easy, not least because of the professional obstacles that have marginalized academic theology. At this point I would like to suggest how these obstacles might be minimized, if not completely eliminated, thereby facilitating the emergence of a more public theology. As I pointed out earlier, professionalization has erected barriers along two fronts: that between the theologian and the general public and that between the theologian and academicians in other fields. The development of a public theology depends upon reconfiguring both boundaries.

Beyond the Academy

The most important factor in communicating to a general educated audience lies in the avoidance of technical language that is only intelligible to comparably trained colleagues. Field specific jargon creates an impregnable barrier in the face of which other changes are simply irrelevant. As we have seen, however, the need to sustain the identity of the professional academician makes changes on this front particularly difficult. We are caught in the "chicken/egg dialectic." The very need for a public theology itself testifies to the power of the countervailing forces. The movement beyond technical jargon in many respects depends upon a transformation in the professional identity of the theologian. For unless that identity is exposed and transformed, the willing appropriation of nontechnical language is unlikely.

Some headway may be made simply by becoming more sensitive to the problem and less tolerant of theological writing that traffics in technical or specialized language. Although such language may be a necessary or useful strategy at times, too often its function is to prop up or to mask what may not stand on its own. I suspect this is often the case when theologians appropriate philosophers and their systems to articulate their views. For every Tillich there are hundreds of others whose selected philosophical systems hide a multidude of sins. Whether the philosopher of choice is Whitehead, Heidegger, or Derrida, theologians should avoid becoming so entrapped in a philosophical system that the uninitiated—which can even be a colleague—cannot hope to break the code. Today it is often difficult to remember that more accessible theologies are not necessarily the popularizations of the theological geniuses. Consider, for instance,

H. Richard Niebuhr's classic work *Radical Monotheism and Western Culture*. This collection of essays epitomizes a public theological style. Niebuhr was able to articulate his distinctive and creative theological perspective without resorting to the specialized discourse which sustains the boundary between the theological expert and the "outsiders."

Those contemporary academic theologies that have been the most successful in communicating to a wider audience have, not surprisingly, reflected commitments beyond the academy. In this they are similar to Luther who was committed to a revitalization movement within the society as a whole. Consider, for instance, feminist theological writings that tend to adopt a rather accessible style, often through the use of first person narrative and experiences. This strategy is both ideologically and practically motivated. The ideological rationale lies in a sense that traditional theological texts and doctrines reflect the historical codification of the experience of men of a certain class. To escape their control feminist theologians seek to mine experiences of "the others" that have been ignored, disvalued, and distorted. This ideological rationale is supplemented by a very pragmatic concern that feminist theology make a difference. Feminist theologians are self-consciously working for the end of patriarchy. This political goal constitutes a commitment located outside the boundaries of the academy. It has encouraged feminist theologians to create forms of theology that are less isolated from the wider society. Daly, Ruether, Christ, and Plaskow, for instance, are read by many who would be hard put to name another leading academic theologian. The same could be said of some other forms of liberation theologies that reflect a commitment beyond the borders of the academy, thereby motivating some, though not all, of these writers to transgress the boundary that separates academic theologians from the general public. These examples underscore the importance of escaping from the mentality that has equated "acting professionally" with neutrality or the transcendence of an advocacy stance.

Beyond the Discipline

By virtue of being engaged in an academic discipline, however, theologians must clearly be concerned with facilitating communication within the academy as well. Only by remaining accountable to other relevant academic inquiries does theology command a similar status. We have already reviewed some of the factors that have contributed to the marginalization of theology within academia. Many of these factors lie beyond the control of those in the field. But not all of them. There are aspects of the traditional genre of theology that need to be reconfigured if theologians are to extend and deepen the liaisons between theology and other forms of academic inquiry.

The most important change, in my judgment, is for theologians to move beyond the boundaries of the text to engage religion as it is embodied in local contexts. Theology, as I am reconfiguring it, engages the religious beliefs and practices of a culture, and in this engagement contributes to their interpretation, evaluation, and reconstruction. To be sure, scripturally based religions cannot be adequately understood without familiarity with the relevant canonical writings. But this reckoning with the text is markedly different from a theology that makes the biblical text or commentaries upon the biblical text its defining source or horizon.

There are a number of reasons for reconfiguring the genre of theology in this way. The first, and most compelling reason, has to do with the desacralization of the Bible during the past few centuries. Without the presumption that the Bible is divinely revealed, the textually based genre of traditional theology loses the premise that legitimated and controlled its form. As we have seen, theology as biblical commentary was driven by the assumption that God's salvific knowledge was somehow associated with this text. But even when theology is no longer biblical commentary, but commentary upon the commentaries upon the commentaries, the implicit assumption running throughout is the revelatory character of the sacred text which anchors the chain.

The rationale for moving beyond the text within theology, however, is not simply a function of the loss of biblical authority. Recent insights into the multivalent meaning and function of religious myths and symbols provide further incentive to engage religion as it is embodied in specific contexts. Within theology these insights have been most forcefully articulated by liberationist theologians who have called our attention to the oppressive meanings and functions of symbols and narratives which, in the abstract, appear harmless, perhaps even edifying. Their work makes clear that the interpretation and evaluation of religious narratives and symbols cannot be prosecuted in abstraction from their instantiation in specific contexts. Far from having static, essential meanings that can be retrieved from a text, they are cultural strategies that cannot be deciphered except through their embodiment in local settings.[27] To return to an earlier chapter's metaphor, the task of contributing the next chapter in a chain novel requires more than textual expertise in the previous chapters, however important that remains. Consider, again, Elisabeth Schüssler Fiorenza's analysis of Christian Scripture and the communities out of which it came. If her argument is correct, some of the earliest chapters in the "chain novel" that is Christianity must be read in light of the patriarchal agenda of its authors. Instead of taking them at face value, contemporary readers and writers must dig beneath their surface to uncover that which was distorted or ignored. The chain novel takes on the character of a detective story, insofar as earlier chapters are read as false clues or deliberate twists to mystify the reader. Perhaps even better than regarding the tradition as a detective story, it is more illuminating to think of it as the recent discovery of many chapters that earlier authors had suppressed. Their surfacing requires the contemporary writer to acknowledge that the novel is far less unified or coherent than earlier chapters had presumed. Such an acknowledgment also underscores the creative contribution of the current writer in his or her attempt to extend the tradition in a manner that takes account of both the need for continuity or fit and the intellectual and moral insights of the writer.[28]

The need to move beyond the text within theology can also be recognized by reconsidering the analogies between theology and judicial reasoning. As we saw in an earlier chapter, judges identify and interpret relevant precedents within the context of specific cases that call for judicial decisions. The identification and interpretation of the precedents is not mechanical, but very much dependent upon application to the particular case under scrutiny. Theological reflection is similarly motivated by application to the contemporary context. However, largely due to the positivistic influence of a particular theory of revelation, the genre of theology has tended to minimize the importance of application in theological reasoning. To continue the analogy, theologians have had limited knowledge of the specifics of the case to which their interpretation applies. Without qualification, however, this point is anachronistic and misleading. Prior to the emergence of modern cultural studies, theologians were forced to rely upon a personal discernment of the "signs of the times." With the rise of modern historical, sociological, and economic studies, however, theologians can achieve a more informed and nuanced understanding of the forces and features that comprise the contemporary situation.

As the genre of theology is reoriented in this fashion, the training and conversation partners for theologians will change commensurately. The nature of theological expertise will be substantially reconfigured. Greater attention to the local embodiment of religious myths, symbols, and practices calls for historical and cultural expertise that has not often been emphasized in theological scholarship. All too often theologians have pursued an ahistorical engagement with the great theologians of the past, regarding them as perennial Christian options rather than as strategies peculiar to a specific place and time. In the contextualization of theology the premium placed on philosophical and exegetical skills would be muted as theologians become more attentive to the interplay between text and context. Interpretation and critique of religious perspectives and behaviors calls for competence in behavioral-explanatory approaches to religion. This line of development would locate theology more deeply and thoroughly in the domain of religious studies, and reduce the gap that currently isolates history of religions from theology. This repositioning would not eliminate the normative and constructive aims of theology by making the history of religions paradigmatic for theological reflection. But it would connect these aims far more closely to the enactment of religion in concrete contexts, thereby curbing the tendency to traffic in ahistorical verities isolated from instantiation in a particular time and place. Critique and construction are not eliminated, then, so much as they are transformed and harnessed more self-consciously to cultural conversations.[29]

Recasting theology in this fashion would also have an impact upon traditional theological sensibilities. The disdain for popular or folk religion, for instance, would be tempered as it became a central focus of attention. Moreover, the antipathy to religious syncretism, an aversion akin to a sense of pollution, would similarly be muted as theologians moved beyond the unifying parameters of a sacred text and immersed themselves in the far messier morass of lived religion.

Extending the genre of theology in this direction would alter the professional boundaries that have increasingly come to insulate theology from both the academy and the wider culture. Following this trajectory would enable theologians to locate their critical and normative reflection within a more thickly developed description of a particular context. The development of this ethnographic expertise would require far greater familiarity with the work of historians and social scientists, thereby minimizing the isolation of professional theologians from other scholars. There is no way to ensure that increased communication between theologians and other scholars would be a two-way street, although I suspect that reconfiguring the genre of theology in this fashion would make it more likely. There is also reason to think that tying theological reflection more closely to the embodiment and enactment of religion in local contexts might help to bridge the gap that separates the professional academic theologian from the wider culture. In this respect, then, reorienting the genre of theology may not only facilitate communication within the academy but beyond it.

Minimizing, let alone overcoming, the professional isolation and insulation of theology is a daunting task. As I have argued in this chapter, however, any success in creating a more public theology depends upon its accomplishment.

Chapter Six

Connecting the Threads

The project to articulate a model for a public theology has been less straightforward than the task may originally have appeared. Rather than simply delineate a form of theology appropriate within public life, we have traveled a more circuitous path that has moved betwixt and between theology and the reigning interpretation of public. In the process it has become apparent that the concept of public is neither as static nor as monochromatic as it might initially have appeared. We have been led to identify and unravel various threads in the prevailing notion of public, considering each in historical context and in relationship to the enterprise of theology. Exploring the concept of public in terms of its various contraries—the parochial, the private, and the professional—has allowed for a more nuanced analysis of public and, by extension, a fuller portrait of a public theology. It has also brought into sharper focus the multiple obstacles and tendencies that function to preclude or impede a public theology.

The problem of a public theology, I have argued, is not simply securing a greater public role for religion. That way of construing the matter, besides failing to distinguish adequately between religion and theology, takes at face value the prevailing typography of public and private life, and attempts to move religion from the private to the public realm. For both methodological and substantive reasons, theology must resist appropriating the current mapping of public and private. Hence in its endeavor to secure a larger, more appropriate public role, theology should simultaneously work for the reconfiguration of the public realm. In many respects theology's very location and status within modernity provide it with the critical perspective and motivation that is needed to dismantle the prevailing paradigm of public that has so effectively marginalized it.

On the other hand, as we have seen, the obstacles to a public theology do not lie entirely in the prevailing interpretation of public. Even with a reinterpretation of the nature of public life and the public exercise of reason, some characteristic features of theology need to be altered if this genre of reflection is to achieve a public status.

This final chapter will reconnect some of the threads of the previous discussion as it reviews the proposed reconfiguration of the public realm and the form of theology most suited to furthering this transformation.

Toward the Transformation of the Public Realm

The Prevailing Topography Revisited

The configuration of the public and private spheres that has come to dominate the modern landscape is characterized by a marked polarization between these realms. Various factors have been cited to account for this development, including the political need to create a "neutral public space" in response to the disruptive early modern religious wars in Europe; the heavy emphasis upon freedom and autonomy to emancipate the individual from the constraints of traditional authorities, including the intrusions of the state; and the influence of empirical, atomistic early modern science in shaping the paradigm of rationality. In and through such influences, the public realm has come to be interpreted in a highly universal albeit exceedingly abstract way. Although it theoretically includes all persons, it is not by virtue of the individual's private history or perspective but by virtue of a rational capacity that is common to all. The consequence is that the individual qua public citizen is rendered identical to and hence interchangeable with all others. This vision of public life is best expressed through quantitative metaphors: the public is the sum of all individuals, each like a cipher whose specificity is immaterial, indeed inappropriate, within public life. Numbers, then, express the autonomy and inter-changeability of the parts, as well as their totality.[1] Private life, on the other hand, has come to demarcate the sphere of the individual and family; this is the realm that contains the personal histories, beliefs, and values that distinguish one self from another.

This way of mapping the differences between private and public life has yielded some enormous gains. It has been instrumental in the formation of modern liberal societies, noted for their enhancement of human freedom, individual rights, and social diversity. And yet despite the beneficial role this vision has played, particularly in the development of Western political and legal institutions, it is highly questionable whether it continues to suffice as an overarching vision of individual and social life. In the previous chapters I have identified some of the limitations of this construal of the public and private realms. The real challenge, however, lies in forging a reconfiguration that overcomes the limitations without sacrificing, in the process, the historic gains in individual rights and freedoms that it has facilitated.

Many of the limitations in the reigning interpretation of the public realm stem from the abstract basis upon which it is constituted, or put differently, from its oppositional location over against the private sphere. The polarization between the private and public spheres renders the former particular and the latter abstract, not inclusive of the differences that are the important and distinguishing features of persons. Public life assumes the character of a vast collectivity. As the sum of all individuals it exists, but it is not something whose nature and quality depend upon the actions of its members. Consequently, it undermines a sense of participatory responsibility in sustaining and transforming this wider life. Moreover, the equality that stems from common membership in public life is formal, irrelevant to the economic and social forms of domination and subordination that shape individual and collective life. Public formal equality, then, coexists far too easily with private inequalities. This vision of public life is powerfully reinforced by a corresponding epistemology and ontology that render it intuitively self-evident.

The epistemological cornerstone of this vision of public life reflects a similar disjunction between the private and public spheres; the former is taken as the provence of subjective ends and values and the latter the domain of objective facts and rationality. From this perspective the public exercise of reason is objective, it deals with facts unhindered and unaffected by private preferences and values. This radical split between fact and value, the objective and the subjective, has spawned a technocratic interpretation of rationality that has contributed to an impoverished public dialogue concerning the ends and values for which individuals and groups act.

It is an epistemology that encourages a sharp distinction between what Thomas McCollough has called official knowledge and personal knowledge. In his words:

> Official knowledge is knowledge that is specialized, technical, and useful. Because of its seemingly objective character, we may forget that it is personal knowledge, validated by our general knowledge and values. . . .Official knowledge will seem to be objective, impersonal, verifiable—public, whereas moral knowledge will seem to be subjective, unverifiable, and private. When this split between knowledge and value is maintained, no effective challenge to official knowledge is possible, nor is there any leverage for a critical moral perspective on public policy making. Official knowledge becomes the property of a ruling elite, whether government or business.[2]

The dichotomy between fact and value that informs this epistemology makes it virtually impossible to interpret public life as a forum within which persons in their concrete specificity engage each other on questions of goals and values. A quantitative calculus is more appropriate for a public life that has relegated values and ends to the private sphere where opinion and emotion reign supreme. The result is a collective inability or refusal to openly and deliberatively explore issues of public concern in terms of moral and religious categories, categories which often remain implicitly operative.

The ontology informing this quantitative vision of the public realm is radically individualistic. Public life is a vast collectivity of interchangeable individual units, rather than an intricately woven fabric of interconnections binding constituent members. Public life is the atomistic individual writ large. The accent is on the freedom and rights of each unit, rather than upon the corresponding contextual constraints and obligations which social membership imposes.

The Communitarian Response

The individualistic orientation that informs this configuration of public life has been a primary feature of the dominant American ethos, embodied in its mythology and encoded in its laws. It is an orientation that has come under increasing scrutiny and criticism from thinkers ranging across a wide ideological spectrum, generating a variety of communitarian antidotes in response. Although these communitarian visions offer important correctives to the individualistic tradition of classical liberalism, a renewed focus upon community can all too easily become a self-legitimizing strategy that justifies concern for "us" at the expense of "them" who stand outside the community. The political economist Robert Reich has recently argued that the emerging focus upon community in the past decade has for the most part been a dangerous and conservative ploy to limit the boundaries of solidarity and obligation. Given economic and social realities in contemporary American society, nostalgic commitment to local geographical communities is all too often a protective strategy to legitimate homogeneous units reflecting similarities in education, income, and race. He writes:

> The renewed emphasis on "community" in American life has justified and legitimized these economic enclaves. If generosity and solidarity end at the border of similarly valued properties, then the most fortunate can be virtuous citizens at little cost. Since most people in one neighborhood or town are equally well off, there is no cause for a guilty conscience.[3]

Indeed the ideology of community, without further qualification in regard to its scope, has served to obscure the
diminishing sense of solidarity within the American polity
as a whole. Celebrating the identity and relative intimacy
of local communities inevitably masks the growing inequalities and divisiveness of the wider society. Economic data
indicate a growing disparity in income levels amongst the
American population. In the past two decades members of
the top income group have increasingly "withdrawn their
dollars from the support of public spaces and institutions
shared by all and dedicated the savings to their own private
services."[4] In some respects this phenomenon is even more
widespread insofar as the suburban middle class in the past
forty years has "withdrawn, geographically and often
mentally, from the challenges of a diverse and unequal
society."[5] Many forms of communitarianism, lacking sufficient
attention to the scope of the community, provide little moral
leverage to challenge these developments.

The growing captivation with communal life has assumed
a religious form as well, contributing to a preoccupation in
many quarters with the character and well-being of the
community of the faithful over against the wider society. The
reaffirmation of the role of particular traditions in shaping
identity and inquiry has provided powerful incentive for
sectarian impulses which do little to elicit a sense of common
life within the society as a whole. The focus, rather, is upon
the concrete meaning, identity, and purpose that a traditioned
religious community facilitates through its particular narratives and symbols.

To safeguard against the self-serving, sectarian potential
in the renewed focus upon community, I have sought instead
to explore the adequacy of the prevailing interpretation of
public to generate commitment to the cultivation of an
inclusive common life. By virtue of connoting the whole, the
concept of public is less easily co-opted to sanction the well-
being of one particular group against the "others." Moreover,
it suggests a way to move beyond the limited options
generated in and through the contrast between community
and society that has dominated recent thinking about social
relations.

Toward a Cosmopolitan Public

It has become common to speak of the emergence of a "global village" in twentieth century life as airplanes, telephones, satellite transmissions, televisions, facsimile machines, and international commercial exchanges bring peoples and cultures together on a far greater scale than ever before in history. As Robert Bellah has noted, one of the greatest problems facing humankind is the need to make this fact of global community come alive politically and morally.[6] To rephrase his observation, I would suggest that our problem lies in more clearly recognizing this rapidly emerging common life and in transforming it into a more genuine communal life.

The interpretation of the public developed in the previous chapters incorporates a global thrust insofar as it stresses a radically inclusive common life, irrespective of geographic and political boundaries. As we have seen, a global public life includes more than the recognition of an interconnected common life; it further incorporates a moral impulse to cultivate a more symmetrical interdependent life. For it is only through adherence to this moral directive within the concept of public life that the problems and threats to the well-being and survival of us all can be addressed. It is this sense of a cosmopolitan public that is demanded by a commitment to truth or, in the nuclear age, survival. But other common endeavors and threats, ranging from economic well-being to terrorism, testify to its critical importance as well.

Reich, for instance, has persuasively argued the appropriateness of a cosmopolitan identity within the emerging global economy that no longer operates according to the dynamics that justified "economic nationalism," the dominant identity of the preceding two centuries. Technological and economic developments have created a far more interconnected world in recent decades, making it increasingly difficult to isolate the well-being of one nation from another, in terms of health, politics, or economics. Consider, for instance, the spread of AIDS or the Chernobyl disaster whose effects know no political or geographical barriers. Similar interdependencies have emerged in the quest for economic well-being, making it far more difficult to separate, say, American economic effects and benefits from those in Japan or Hong Kong. Such developments strongly suggest that "life on this planet has become less a set of contests in which one party can be victorious, and more an intricate set of relationships which either succeed or fail—we win or we lose together."[7] Developing a global identity reflecting a commitment to an inclusive public life, then, is fast becoming indispensable to our individual and collective well-being.

On the other hand, despite the critical importance of cultivating a global public life and identity, such cosmopolitanism is insufficient in and of itself. For reasons that will be explored below, cosmopolitanism must be rooted in and refracted through more local associations. The primacy of nations in the formation of identity and the exercise of power makes attention to this level of societal life especially important.

American Public Life

However essential a cosmopolitan sense of public life has become, in and of itself it is an inadequate basis for the formation of personal identity and meaning. It is too abstract, too divorced from actual societies with their highly idiosyncratic histories and mythologies. That humans require a far more particular identity, located concretely in space and time, has become increasingly apparent in the face of the growing resurgence in ethnic, regional, and religious affiliations. Vast collectivities based upon very thin, abstract commonalities seem unable to replace local associations with their richly textured, highly particular cultures. Attention to a specifically American public life, then, acknowledges the additional need for social identities more circumscribed than the global.

Attention to national life is also required in light of the social and political configurations of the contemporary world. Nations today are the social units that wield primary power within the global arena. Because military, economic, social, and political decisions are made at the national level, not at the global level, it is essential to have a public life within which such decisions can be debated and held accountable.

These reasons, among others, make clear that an American public life has intrinsic value; it ought not to be regarded as simply an obstacle to a global public life. The tension and relationship between these forms of public life will be considered more fully below.

Many of the problems plaguing contemporary American life are exacerbated, indeed reinforced, by the prevailing form of public life that we have been examining in this study. I do not mean to suggest, of course, that they are all caused by this social model, or that serious oppression, ranging from the economic to the racial, could be eradicated simply by its reconfiguration. My point, rather, is that some headway, however modest, can be made by working toward the trans-formation of the public realm within which these problems are rooted and addressed.

Over against the prevailing model of public life recapitu-lated above, this study has sketched out an alternative perspective that avoids its individualistic, quantitative, and anthropocentric tendencies. Put briefly, the proposed alter-native abandons the vision of public life as a collection of atomistic individuals in favor of a view which underscores the interconnections and interdependencies of all life forms. Without denying the reality and value of individuals, it refocuses attention upon the common life within which they exist. This refocusing does not eliminate the diversity of individual interests and ends, but it locates them within a larger context of shared interests and values. Moreover, it highlights the extent to which these shared interests and values are increasingly indispensable to the survival and well-being of us all. Hence the contemporary exigency to develop an ethos that encourages the sustaining and nurturing of this common life. The sharp opposition between the interests and ends of the individual and the common good, the dichotomy that has fueled the liberal trajectory, has come to the end of its social utility, its emancipatory power eroded.

Moving toward this reconstruction of public life within the American context would temper the growing atomization within the society as a whole. In the past couple of decades this atomization has become less a form of rugged individualism than a fragmentation into special interest groups, each preoccupied with advancing its claims and demands upon the polity as a whole. The language of rights and entitlements dominates the rhetoric of each group, with little attention to shared obligations and responsibilities. The fracturing of American society into a special interest pluralism has impeded the emergence of any enduring sense of "us" within the nation, one, that is, that is not simply a function of a wartime unity over against a foreign enemy.

Romantic nostalgia for some earlier unity is not appropriate either, of course, given the slave society of earlier centuries and the enduring legacy of white supremacy. This is not, then, a restoration project, a point white Americans can all too easily overlook. It is, rather, an effort to cultivate a realistic sense of a common life that does not thereby obliterate the ways in which differentials of power perpetuate forms of domination and subordination. Currently, the interests of each group are typically put forth in isolation from the underlying layer of common interests and endeavors that are also necessary for the survival and well-being of each. This strategy is entirely appropriate given a view of public life as the arena within which special interest groups jockey for power.[8] Operating out of this interpretation of public life and democratic pluralism effectively masks, and gradually erodes, the underlying commonalities and shared interests of the various constituencies. The remedy is not simply to silence the critical voices of various constituencies but to facilitate a sense of a more encompassing life that binds us all together. Within this broader framework the existence of shared goals that entail mutual responsibilities and obligations will become more visible. This perspective does not falsify the concerns of each interest group but shows them to be partial truths.

It is especially important to recognize the extent to which this form of public life can work for rather than against legitimate claims of the various groups. At issue is the question as to how claims can be most persuasively made. Political commentators have begun to note the growing indifference, even resistance, to some of the more militant claims voiced by various constituencies. Political tactics which exacerbate the fragmentation within American society may be inadvertently contributing to the erosion of any sense of solidarity that might be tapped to respond positively to the challenges. In political columnist Meg Greenfield's words:

> You can only harangue people and tell them what bad guys and oppressors they are and that they have a debt and better make good on it for so long before they tell you to get lost. Especially as those groups that have been victimized because of race or gender or other characteristics have come to champion their own causes militantly, it has become harder to persuade those they are challenging or sometimes denouncing that they need to fulfill a duty of penance for the past. Only some genuine feeling of connection and mutual interest and shared purpose can any longer cause them to respond or even to believe they have obligations of this kind.[9]

Taking a more historical view of the economic and political transformations in twentieth century America, Reich, too, describes an alarming loss of solidarity within the nation. During the economic boom of the sixties and early seventies the ramifications of this loss were tempered by the easy money available for charity to "them," the outsiders in American society. However, with the economic downturn, altruism has lost its political allure. The most pressing need within our society is the cultivation of a sense of "us" to replace the increasingly ineffective appeals to charity and altruism.[10] Only such a collective self-understanding can provide a basis, deep enough to endure through economic cycles, and powerful enough to motivate the ongoing struggle for a more just society.

A Polymorphous Public Life: Identity and Pluralism

The proposed reinterpretation of public life may initially appear contradictory insofar as both a global and national form of public life are endorsed. To understand how both can be affirmed simultaneously without serious contradiction leads us into a complex of issues concerning the nature of personal identity as well as the relationship between the concrete and the universal. Attending to these issues, even if briefly, also provides a rather different perspective on the nature of the public realm, serving in some important ways as a corrective to the foregoing analysis.

The preoccupation with the nature and importance of the public sphere in this study can all too easily foster the impression that the individual is purely an abstraction or that individual identity is entirely a product of a radically inclusive public life. Not only do such inferences seriously misconstrue the nature of individual identity but they distort the form of public life proposed herein. It would appear important, then, to consider more explicitly than I have done thus far the issue of personal identity in the proposed rein-terpretation of the public realm. Although this issue is far more complex than these concluding remarks can suggest, its centrality to a more adequate drawing of the private and public spheres warrants its consideration.

Perhaps the simplest and most basic point is to reiterate the importance of the individual in his or her particularity to the formation of a public life. By mitigating the sharp opposition between the private and public realm, the proposed reinterpretation of public life, far from undermining the status or significance of the individual, seeks to do the opposite.[11] Construing the public realm as an interconnected network of relational beings renders particular identity more decisive, not less so. Public life is not an amorphous collec-tivity but the intricate web of intersecting private histories that bind selves and societies into finely woven tapestries. This form of public life, then, is not generated by abstracting from concrete embodied beings but by recognizing their embeddedness in a more inclusive common life.

That a viable public life could be created and sustained by evading particularity has been, as we have seen, a fundamental tenet of the prevailing model. It was forged out of the desperate need and hope to transcend the conflicts spawned by particular religious and ethnic affiliations. The emancipatory, irenic, and universal impulses of this vision of public life are indisputable and have been critical to the formation of modern Western societies. Nevertheless, it has become increasingly important to reckon with the limitations, and inherent instability, of this model. The developments occurring, for instance, in Eastern Europe and the former Soviet Union raise basic questions about modern experiments to create vast unions that circumvent local sources of identity and meaning. Repeatedly we are seeing peoples reaffirm their particular ethnic and religious heritages in lieu of the more amorphous collectivities in which unity is a function of an abstract commonality. The resurgent fundamentalisms around the globe further reinforce the perception that the local and traditional sources of meaning remain critical for individual identity.

It is impossible to witness the reaffirmation of identity through particular ethnic and religious affiliations without apprehension about the potential divisiveness of this historical trend. In the light of modern technological capabilities this trajectory appears especially ominous. The challenge of our age would seem to lie in the formation of a public life that encompasses, rather than excludes, particularity. At this historic juncture we either find a way to reappropriate particular traditions and local associations within a more inclusive public order, or risk a return to conflicts that are fueled by ethnic and religious loyalties. The previous chapters have sought to address this challenge by advocating a more polymorphous form of public life. But it is critical to recognize that this form of public life calls for a perennial reorientation in the identity of the individual and social units that are its constituent elements. A viable public life is not simply a composite of the multitudinous traditions and associations that currently flourish. Equating public life with this sort of pastiche snapshot ignores the moral and social struggle that the formation of public life requires, thereby intimating that the reconfiguration of public life is the result of a definitional fiat. Greater attention to the formation of individual identity illuminates the nature and direction of the perennial struggle that the cultivation and transformation of a more adequate public life demands.

Individual identity that is located within bounded communities, construed as the ultimate source of meaning and value, is far different from the identity generated from the attempt to situate primary communities within a more comprehensive communal order. Commitment to a global community demands that identity for individuals and societies reflect a dual allegiance to both a particular history within which identity and meaning have been rooted and the global order which remains to be fully actualized. H. Richard Niebuhr offers a particularly penetrating analysis of this sort of dual allegiance in his exploration of radical monotheism. A radically monotheistic stance, which for Niebuhr reflects a commitment to a universal order, does not eliminate finite sources of meaning and value; rather it creates a perpetual revolution within them and within the individual whose identity is constituted by them. In his words, "Faith in God involves us in a permanent revolution of the mind and of the heart, a continuous life which opens out infinitely into ever new possibilities."[12] More recently, Charles Davis has explored the sort of identity that is newly demanded in face of the incipient signs of an emerging global order. Like Niebuhr, Davis seeks to retain the tension and dialectic between the local extant associations and traditions and the universal. He writes:

> Human history has become one in a conscious and active way, so that a social identity that is not anachronistic has to be grounded upon a collective reality wider than that of the particular State. There is, indeed, not yet a universal, global order, but there is the opportunity of participating in its emergence by evoking the inherently universal structure of communication to shape a new collective will, leading to an order beyond the present divisions. However much we may positively value a particular national heritage, possessing it as a fixed and finished whole cannot ground a rational social identity today. Instead, that heritage must serve as a source of a distinctive contribution

to the common enterprise of forming a new, complex and universal identity for people of all nations.[13]

Davis's formulation of the nature of identity in an emerging global order, perhaps due to its Habermasian overtones, does tend to downplay the continued role of local traditions in the formation of universal identity. Despite this tendency, Davis helps to clarify the historical conditions that make both possible and necessary the reformulation of identity within an emerging global order. Although using different language, Davis underscores the double consciousness that must attend the formation of identity if this development is to be effected. While particular communities and traditions remain critical in shaping identity, they are not taken as "fixed and finished wholes" but as indispensable but evolving vehicles for a more inclusive order. Membership in such entities is experienced as a "point of entry" to a wider conversation and to a larger shared task of creating a global community. Thus we can see that the creation of a polymorphous public life is not achieved simply by pasting together particular traditions and communities with their dispositions to exclusivity and superiority. On the contrary, the particular traditions and associations must undergo a perennial internal revolution if the emergence of a more global community is to be effected. An earlier chapter's attempt to formulate a more adequate interpretation of God from a Christian perspective is indicative of the kind of "insider" revisions that are needed to facilitate the relocation of particular traditions within a more inclusive common life. A similar reworking of the dominant myths that have informed American life is needed to break down their imperialistic and exclusive tendencies that work against the formation of a more encompassing and more just global order. Given the strongly religious character of these myths, much of this critique and reconstruction can be profitably pursued from a theological perspective.

Referring to the formation of identity within an emerging global order as a function of a double consciousness must now be qualified. Although the expression illuminates the dialectic between the particular and the universal, it obscures the complexity of this relationship and hence offers too simplistic a portrait of individual identity. We are, of course, not members of only one community or tradition that serves as our exclusive "point of entry" to the cultivation of a global order. We belong to a variety of social units each with its own history and agenda. Nor is the image of the onion with each layer occupying an appropriate location within the whole an adequate picture. That image is far too neat, suggesting that there is some proper order that can eliminate the tensions and conflicting loyalties generated by our membership in the differing associations. Consider that a single individual is often a member of a family, a neighborhood, town, state, occupation, nation, ethnic group, and religious community. Not only is there no overarching coherent order within which each of these associations can be located, but the social units themselves are marked by varying degrees of tension and discord. The individual, then, is perennially involved in synthesizing the competing values and demands within these associations as well as between them. The synthesis is never neat; it may approximate a pragmatic working but never, for extended periods, a rationally coherent resolution to the conflicts. Hence the synthesis is forged against the backdrop of real loss, even tragedy, as competing goods and values must be sacrificed to others. The double consciousness that emerges from a commitment to a global order does not generate resolutions for all the conflicts, but it does transform the identity of those engaged in struggling with them. It makes vividly clear that the creation of public life is a perennial task with an inescapably moral dimension to it.

The Contribution of a Public Theology

As the previous chapters have argued, religion and theology have enormous potential to contribute to the reconfiguration of the prevailing model of public life. This is not to deny their complicity, even if originally involuntary, in sustaining the reigning paradigm. Nor is it to deny the necessary involvement of other factors in effecting social change. But it is to suggest that religious resources, if appropriately and effectively used, can play a significant motivational and explanatory role in rewriting the "myth of liberalism" that plays such a fundamental role in sustaining the prevailing model of public life.

One of the burdens of this study has been to demonstrate the substantive theological reasons for reconfiguring the culturally dominant vision of public life. These reasons are most evident in a consideration of the meaning and ramifications of commitment to God. Properly interpreted, the inherited stories of God offer powerful support for a more communal, inclusive interpretation of public life. The universal implications of the symbolism of God the Creator facilitate a commitment to the whole interconnected web of being, and the normative ramifications of the biblical stories of a just and loving God provide a critical angle on common life as it is currently constituted, thereby eliciting an impetus to work towards its transformation. Although this interpretation of God emerges from a particular discernment of the needs and problems of the current moment, it is not thereby simply a pragmatic reworking of, in this case, Christianity to solve a societal problem. That way of putting the matter fails to recognize the extent to which this interpretation of God is deeply embedded in the Christian tradition. The retrieval of this theological trajectory is governed by its application, analogous, as we have seen, to judicial interpretation. Nonetheless, it is a reading and extension of the tradition that has both historical and moral justification.

Beyond the Role of Caretaker

Although Christianity offers substantive support for the transformation of our vision of public life, it is important that this support not be undermined by the very form of reflection used to commend it. Theologians, in other words, should argue for the revisioning of public life in a genuinely public manner. This methodological stricture continues to challenge the public status of much theological reflection.

I have already alluded to the disturbing trend in contemporary theology in which a "postmodern" critique of the modern epoch is used to defend what amounts to a modern-day version of fideism. The growing popularity of this theological movement does not bode well for the emergence of a more public form of theology. Moreover, it is a movement whose appeal and power are all the more potent because of the accuracy of its criticisms of the prevailing interpretation of the public exercise of rationality with its pretensions to ahistorical objectivity. But it deploys these criticisms to advance a position which, in my judgment, severs critical ties to the public realm. This movement's legitimate and important reaffirmation of particularity leads not to the reconfiguration of the public realm but to its abandonment.

Moreover, it justifies this reaffirmation of particularity with very traditional assumptions concerning the nature and source of religious truth. Consider in this regard the observations of William Placher who undertakes a careful assessment of the positions of "revisionist" theologians and "postliberal" theologians; the former seek to engage Christianity in the public conversation, whereas the latter are especially concerned to preserve the distinctiveness of Christianity. His remarks are especially revealing because of his recognition of the excesses of the postliberal alternative, and his resulting desire to bridge the gap between these two camps. He writes:

> Revisionist theologians are trying to get Christian theology involved in the public conversations of our culture. It is a laudable aim. Their strategies for accomplishing that end, however, risk cutting and trimming the gospel to fit it to the categories and assumptions of a particular philosophical or cultural position.[14]

On the surface this observation seems so reasonable, so balanced, that its assumption about religious truth is liable to go undetected. The assumption grows more visible, and hopefully more troubling, when located within a different context. Consider, then, a paraphrase of this observation without its gospel reference. Imagine, say, a philosopher writing:

Revisionist philosophers are trying to get Platonic philosophy involved in the public conversations of our culture. It is a laudable aim. Their strategies for accomplishing that end, however, risk cutting and trimming Plato's philosophy to fit it to the categories and assumptions of a particular religious or cultural position.

Fellow philosophers would surely find that sort of worry very odd, misplaced within a philosophical discussion. But many theologians, it seems to me, remain preoccupied with precisely this sort of worry. And that I take to be a telling sign, indicative of the distance that continues to separate the genre of theology from more public forms of reflection. For the willingness to risk transformation in encounters with alternative traditions and inquiries, both religious and secular, is surely an indispensable mark of the public exercise of reason, successful attacks on the pretensions to universal and objective rationality notwithstanding.

Theology will only become accepted within the university if the role of the theologian ceases being primarily that of "caretaker" of religion.[15] In my judgment it is critical that the genre of theology, in at least one of its trajectories, pursue this path beyond the "caretaker" role. Failure to do so will simply perpetuate the prevailing pattern within higher education which, if no longer excluding religion from its purview, domesticates it by refusing to engage it on issues of truth and reality.

The emergence of departments of religious studies, largely a post–World War II phenomenon in the United States, did not overturn the prevailing assumption that religion is a private affair, a matter of faith (or opinion) but surely not reason. As religion has entered the curriculum it has been subject to the constraints of the reigning university ethos that is dominated by the Enlightenment model of rationality. Moreover, in their haste to distance themselves from association with traditional theology, scholars of religion have tended to embrace this ethos enthusiastically. Hence the description, analysis, and comparison of religions have been championed to the exclusion of any, at least overt, assessment of them.

To deal with religions on the level of truth claims about reality has continued to be anathema to most religionists who remain far more comfortable in their descriptive abode. Indeed to ask about the truth claims implicit in religions is all too often considered a thinly disguised imperialistic strategy, and rejected for a descriptive cultural relativism, invariably put forth as the moral high road. Given the traditional mode within which religious truth has been explored, it is hardly surprising that scholars of religion would shy away from it altogether—theologians have no claim to the moral high road either. But avoiding normative inquiries in religion is not a solution either. Consider what this evasion fosters.

First, it removes critical assessment of religion—one of the more powerful forces shaping human thought and action—from the realm of disciplined reflection whose primary institutional location in contemporary society is the university. By virtue of this exclusion, religion is not subject to the critical public exploration that such a powerful cultural force surely demands. But this exclusion is, somewhat ironically, a double-edged sword. On the one hand, the status of religion is undermined insofar as its claims are not taken seriously within the public realm, the domain that lays claim to objectivity. On the other hand, the association of religion with a private faith or personal experience grants it far too much unexamined power. From this angle, then, its marginalized location renders it a force that remains largely outside the bounds of critical reflection.

Excluding normative inquiries in religion from the university curriculum is symptomatic of the more general failure of contemporary society to engage in public exploration about the nature of the good life for the individual and the society. Edward Farley describes this as "the failure of the university to formulate education as a paideia, an ideal of the educated person."[16] He attributes this failure to the technological mind-set of contemporary western society which, we have seen, is bound up with the prevailing model of the public exercise of reason. Echoing this point Martha Nussbaum notes:

There's a real danger that we're becoming a nation of narrowly technical thinkers, and losing the sense of the richness and the multifacetedness of the good life that the heritage from Greece gives us. To lose that is to lose the opportunity to have an effective public culture. If we don't start thinking with imagination about the different parts of the good human life and what it is to make a citizen capable of functioning in all these areas, then we're in danger of losing any chance to make good lives for our people.[17]

As Nussbaum reminds us, exploring the ancient Greek conversation about the good life is not pursued for some antiquarian scholarly interest, but for the enrichment and challenge to our own perceptions about what makes for the well-being of individuals and societies. But there is no reason to limit this conversation to ancient Greek culture and religion. Other religions and cultures, also, are rich cultural deposits for analogous perceptions. A critical engagement with Aristotle and Plato is no different, certainly no more academic or public, than a critical engagement with Augustine and Confucius, prevailing disciplinary boundaries notwithstanding.

The genre of theology, properly transformed, has the potential to reintegrate into the university curriculum disciplined analysis and debate concerning religious perceptions of the self, society, and the cosmos. In the previous chapter I suggested that the needed transformation of theology lies in the direction of a closer engagement between theologians and the field of religious studies. It is equally critical to recognize the distinctive contribution that theology can bring to the academic study of religion. By failing to engage in the critical reflection upon religion in a genuinely public, open fashion, theologians relinquish the opportunity to bring religion as a living voice, rather than a dead artifact, back into the cultural conversation centered within the university.

Concluding Note

There are, of course, antecedents within American religious thought for the form of theological reflection advocated herein. The vision of public theology developed in this work stands within a historical line of thinkers whose writings on religion forge a distinctive tradition of American religious reflection that I have sought in various ways to appropriate and extend. Although an extensive historical reconstruction of this lineage lies beyond the scope of this study, its identification tempers the free-floating aura that this systematic portrait of public theology inevitably exudes.[18] Public theology, despite the recent currency of the label, continues an orientation that can be traced back through several generations of American religious thinkers. Although increasingly overshadowed by fideistic and neo-Barthian forms of religious thought, this theological trajectory deserves renewed attention in the struggle to reverse the cultural marginalization of the genre.

By my reckoning this tradition of American religious reflection first comes to clear expression in the writings of the turn of the century American thinker Josiah Royce; includes such earlier twentieth century figures as Walter Rauschenbusch and the Niebuhr brothers; and currently finds expression in the writings of, for instance, Gordon Kaufman and James Gustafson.[19] Although first and primarily a Protestant theological tradition, it has begun to assume a Roman Catholic shape as well, reflected, for instance, in the writings of John Courtney Murray, Rosemary Ruether, and John Coleman as well as the recent American Catholic bishops' letters on nuclear warfare and economic justice. With the emergence of a Roman Catholic variant of this perspective, it is impossible to speak of a single line of historical influence. Although responding to the pressures and concerns of differing eras, these various writers share an affinity in regard to the method, substance, and style of many of their writings on religion. It is an affinity most clearly and fully captured in the label "public."

The notion of public religion or public theology is to most American ears puzzling if not outright subversive and dangerous, with echoes of fundamentalism, totalitarianism, and theocracy ringing in the background. Part of the burden of this study has been to show how religion and theology can

move outside the private realm without necessarily leading
to the suppression of religious freedom, or the abridgement
of the separation between the church and the state. A public
theology, as I have delineated it, does not seek the official
establishment of a single religion, or the elimination of the
multiplicity of religious traditions that mark the contemporary American landscape. It is not part of a larger
Durkheimian project that seeks one religion for one people
in an effort to create social unity. On the contrary, public
theology draws upon the resources of a particular religious
tradition to establish a deeper sense of a common public life
that demands commitment and nurturing in order to enhance
human life and flourishing for both the self and the wider
society. Through this task, which it executes in the spirit of
open inquiry, it contributes to the ideological and practical
reconfiguration of the public realm, thereby witnessing to the
understanding that "faith in God cannot become incarnate
except in a universal community in which all walls of
partition have been broken down."[20] The utopian ring to this
faith ought not to blind us to its pragmatic value as we
respond to the challenge to create a more just and peaceable
order for the religiously, culturally, and racially diverse
societies of the twenty-first century.

Notes

Chapter 1.

1. See, for example, Johannes B. Metz, *Theology of the World,* trans. William Glen Doepel (New York: Herder and Herder, 1969) and *Faith in History and Society,* trans. David Smith (New York: Seabury, 1980); Jurgen Moltmann, *Theology of Hope,* trans. James W. Leitch (London: SCM Press, 1967).

2. Richard John Neuhaus, *The Naked Public Square: Religion and Democracy in America* (Grand Rapids, Mich.: Eerdmans, 1984), 80.

3. Neuhaus, *The Naked Public Square,* 86. See also Neuhaus, "From Civil Religion to Public Philosophy," in *Civil Religion and Political Theology,* ed. Leroy S. Rouner (South Bend, Ind.: University of Notre Dame Press, 1986), 105-6.

4. Bellah's writings on this topic include the following: Bellah, *The Broken Covenant* (New York: Seabury Press, 1975); Robert Bellah and Phillip Hammond, *Varieties of Civil Religion* (San Francisco: Harper and Row, 1980); Bellah, "Public Philosophy and Public Theology in America Today," in *Civil Religion and Political Theology,* ed. Leroy S. Rouner; Bellah et al., *Habits of the Heart: Individualism and Commitment in American Life* (Berkeley: University of California Press, 1985).

5. David Tracy, *The Analogical Imagination* (New York: Crossroads, 1981), 13.

6. Max L. Stackhouse, "An Ecumenist's Plea for a Public Theology," *This World* 8 (1984): 54. For a fuller development of Stackhouse's understanding of public theology, see *Public Theology and Political Economy: Christian Stewardship in Modern Society* (Grand Rapids, Mich.: Eerdmans, 1987).

171

172	*Notes*

7. William James, *Varieties of Religious Experience* (New York: Macmillan Publishing Company, 1961), 42. Although James makes very clear that his definition of religion is pragmatic, a heuristic device for the purposes of his particular study, he clearly stands within an intellectual and cultural tradition that has made private religious experience paradigmatic for religion.

8. For a very illuminating historical overview of the meaning and contrast between public and private in Western culture, with particular attention to the role and status of women, see Jean Bethke Elshtain, *Public Man, Private Woman: Women in Social and Political Thought* (Princeton: Princeton University Press, 1981). See also Zillah R. Eisenstein, *The Radical Future of Liberal Feminism* (New York: Longman, 1981) and Carole Pateman, "Feminist Critiques of the Public/Private Dichotomy," in *Public and Private in Social Life*, eds. S. I. Benn and G. F. Gaus (New York: St. Martin's Press, 1983).

9. See, for example, Richard Sennett's *The Fall of Public Man* (New York: Knopf, 1977) for an interesting study of the transformations within the last few centuries of the contours and meaning of the public realm as reflected in changing styles of architecture, dress, and behavior. Susan Brownmiller explores some of the transformations in dress and aesthetic ideal for women in *Femininity* (New York: Simon and Schuster, 1984).

10. The following analysis of Greek life draws upon Hannah Arendt's study *The Human Condition* (Chicago: University of Chicago Press, 1958). See, especially, the section entitled "The Public and the Private Realm," 22–78. See also Elshtain, *Public Man, Private Woman*, 11–16. Elshtain is especially good at countering the tendency to romanticize Greek public life. As she notes, it was not only an exclusive preserve but it rested upon a negative assessment of the value of the private realm.

11. The Greek conception of the "polis" referred to that public space within which citizens revealed their "unique identities through action and speech" in the process of debating and administering the affairs of a common life. For a discussion of the polis in ancient Greek life, particularly as it informs Arendt's philosophy, see Peter Fuss, "Hannah Arendt's Conception of Political Community," in *Hannah Arendt: The Recovery of the Public World*, ed. Melvyn A. Hill (New York: St. Martin's Press, 1979), 157–76.

Notes

173

12. Arendt, *The Human Condition*, 29. See also Gerda Lerner, *The Creation of Patriarchy* (New York: Oxford University Press, 1985), 199–211.

13. Hannah Arendt, *Between Past and Future* (New York: Viking Press, 1954), 104–9.

14. Arendt, *The Human Condition*, 38. See also Ralph Ketcham, *Individualism and Public Life* (New York: Basil Blackwell, 1987), 33–37.

15. Arendt, *The Human Condition*, 38.

16. Ibid., 65.

17. The classic statement of this position is found in Thomas Hobbes' *Leviathan* (London: Basil Blackwell, 1946).

18. Paraphrase of a sentence by R. W. K. Hinton, "Was Charles I a Tyrant?" *Review of Politics*, vol. 18 (January 1956), quoted in Arendt, *The Human Condition*, 68.

19. See, for example, Richard H. Popkin, *The History of Skepticism from Erasmus to Spinoza* (Berkeley: University of California Press, 1979), 1–17 and Jeffrey Stout, *The Flight from Authority: Religion, Morality and the Quest for Autonomy* (South Bend: University of Notre Dame Press, 1981), 41–49.

20. For a fuller discussion of the relationship between philosophical liberalism and early modern capitalism, see Ketcham, *Individualism and Public Life*, 48–54.

21. William M. Sullivan, *Reconstructing Public Philosophy* (Berkeley: University of California Press, 1986), 60.

22. Ibid., 64.

23. This, of course, was not the position of all Enlightenment theorists, as, for instance, Kant's writings make clear. Although Kant did not consider moral judgments a form of knowledge, they were a function of the practical employment of reason, and hence not irrational or subjective. Nevertheless, the effects of Kant's distinction between pure and practical reason contributed significantly to the gradual relegation of religion, morality, and aesthetics to a noncognitive status.

24. For a very illuminating study of the forces within modernity which have contributed to an instrumentalist conception of reason

and an atomistic anthropology, see Charles Taylor, *The Sources of the Self* (Cambridge: Harvard University Press, 1989).

25. Iris Murdoch in *The Sovereignty of Good* (New York: Schocken Books, 1970) explores the impact of this development upon moral philosophy.

26. Hans-Georg Gadamer has explored the Enlightenment's "prejudice against prejudice" in his *Truth and Method*, trans. and ed. Garrett Harden and John Cumming (New York: Seabury, 1975), 245–53.

27. Thomas Luckmann, *The Invisible Religion: The Problem of Religion in Modern Society* (New York: Macmillan, 1967), 97.

28. Sennett, *The Fall of Public Man*, 4.

29. Ibid., 5.

30. Josiah Royce, *The Basic Writings of Josiah Royce*, vol. 2, ed. John J. McDermott (Chicago: University of Chicago Press, 1969), 1074.

31. See, for example, Josiah Royce, *The Problem of Christianity* (Chicago: University of Chicago Press, 1968), 110–14, 126–30; Royce, "Provincialism" in *The Basic Writings of Josiah Royce*, 1074–88; John Dewey, *Individualism: Old and New* (New York: Capricorn Books, 1929), 74–100.

32. John Dewey, *The Public and Its Problems* (Chicago: Swallow Press, 1927), 67.

33. Ibid., 208.

34. Arendt, *The Human Condition*, 57.

35. Similar efforts can be found in the writings of more recent theorists. See, for example: Richard Bernstein, "The Meaning of Public Life," in *Religion and American Public Life*, ed. Robin W. Lovin (New York: Paulist Press, 1986); Sullivan, *Reconstructing Public Philosophy*; and William Lee Miller, *The First Liberty: Religion and the American Republic* (New York: Knopf, 1986).

36. Those familiar with Habermas's writings will recognize the Habermasian overtones of these conceptions of public and rationality which inform his critical theory. Richard Bernstein has explored the similarities between Arendt and Habermas on these issues in "The Meaning of Public Life."

37. Challenging the public/private geography that we have inherited can also take the form of disputing the value of the categories "public" and "private" to make sense of contemporary life. Christopher Lasch, for instance, pursues this alternative in "The Communitarian Critique of Liberalism," *Soundings* 69:1/2 (1986): 60–76.

38. Roland A. Delattre, "The Culture of Procurement: Reflections on Addiction and the Dynamics of American Culture," *Soundings* 69:1/2 (1986): 143.

39. Recent analyses of the composite character of American society include Sullivan, *Reconstructing Public Philosophy*; Bellah et al., *Habits of the Heart*; and Miller, *The First Liberty: Religion and the American Republic*.

40. Sullivan, *Reconstructing Public Philosophy*, 4.

41. Quoted in Theodore Draper, "Hume and Madison: The Secrets of Federalist Paper No. 10," *Encounter* 58 (1982): 47; cited in Bellah et al., *Habits of the Heart*, 254.

42. Miller, *The First Liberty*, 345.

43. Alexis de Tocqueville, *Democracy in America* vol. I, trans. Henry Reeve, ed. Phillips Bradley (New York: Vintage Books, 1945), 316.

44. Cited in Miller, *The First Liberty*, 244.

45. Miller, *The First Liberty*, 245.

46. *Newsweek*, July 6, 1987, 8.

47. John A. Coleman, *An American Strategic Theology* (New York: Paulist Press, 1982), 60.

48. In *Tales of A New America* (New York: Times Books, 1987) the political economist Robert B. Reich offers a fascinating analysis of the dominant myths that have shaped American society and which continue to provide the parameters for contemporary American politics in both its liberal and conservative variants. His study is especially interesting for demonstrating the continuing power of moral and religious assumptions and values in shaping public life despite their supposed exclusion as per the prevailing ideology. The consequence is a failure to explore these deeper assumptions and values that continue to mold the American identity.

49. For a historical review of the relationship between religion, especially Protestantism, and individualism, see Ketcham, *Individualism and Public Life*, 37–54. See also Harold Bloom, *The American Religion* (New York: Simon and Schuster, 1992).

50. Leroy S. Rouner, "To Be at Home: Civil Religion as Common Bond," in *Civil Religion and Political Theology*, 131–32.

51. John F. Wilson, "Common Religion in American Society," in *Civil Religion and Political Theology*, 122.

52. Martin Marty, *The Public Church*, (New York: Crossroads, 1981), 16.

53. Edward Farley, *Ecclesial Reflection: An Anatomy of Theological Method* (Philadelphia: Fortress Press, 1982), 112. Farley develops a very detailed and persuasive case for the authoritarian mode of classical theology in this study. Although providing a fascinating exposé of the "house of authority," his phenomenologically rooted proposal for the future of theology is, in my judgment, far less compelling. Nevertheless, the limitations of his constructive alternative in no way undermine the cogency of his historical reconstruction and evaluation of classical Christian theology.

Chapter 2.

1. The position I am developing shares the postmodern rejection of the ahistorical, non-traditioned construal of rationality that has animated the Enlightenment project. However, I am reluctant to appropriate the label "postmodernism" for my project because of my increasing dissatisfaction with the oppositionally defined categories of "modernism" and "postmodernism." I have attempted to clarify my uneasiness with the way these categories divide up the contemporary landscape in "Resisting the Postmodern Turn: Theology and Contextualization" in *Theology at the End of Modernity*, ed. Sheila Greeve Davaney (Philadelphia: Trinity Press International, 1991), 81–98.

2. David Tracy, *The Analogical Imagination: Christian Theology and the Culture of Pluralism* (New York: Crossroad, 1981), 51.

3. Tracy's understanding of fundamental theology is developed most fully in *Blessed Rage for Order* (New York: Seabury, 1975) and of systematic theology in *The Analogical Imagination*.

4. David Tracy, "Defending the Public Character of Theology," *The Christian Century* (April 1, 1981): 352.

5. Tracy, "Defending the Public Character of Theology," 353.

6. Tracy, *The Analogical Imagination*, 132.

7. Tracy, *The Analogical Imagination*, 63.

8. For more recent philosophical arguments against the Enlightenment model of reason, see, for example, Richard Rorty, *Philosophy and the Mirror of Nature* (Princeton: Princeton University Press, 1979); Richard J. Bernstein, *Beyond Objectivism and Relativism* (Philadelphia: University of Pennsylvania Press, 1983); Hilary Putnam, *Reason, Truth and History* (Cambridge: Cambridge University Press, 1981).

9. For similar criticisms of the conservative implications of this theological model, see John Cobb's review of *The Analogical Imagination* in *Religious Studies Review* 7/4 (October 1981): 283; Gordon Kaufman, "Conceptualizing Diversity Theologically," *The Journal of Religion* 62/4 (October 1982): 397; and Elisabeth Schüssler Fiorenza, *Bread Not Stone* (Boston: Beacon, 1984), xvi, 9–10.

10. The emphasis upon a "hermeneutics of suspicion" is even more pronounced in his later work *Plurality and Ambiguity: Hermeneutics, Religion, Hope* (San Francisco: Harper and Row, 1987).

11. See, for example, the well-known arguments by two philosophers of science: Paul Feyerabend, *Against Method: Outline of an Anarchistic Theory of Knowledge* (London: NLB, 1975) and Thomas Kuhn, *The Structure of Scientific Revolutions* (Chicago: University of Chicago Press, 1970). Although a historicist interpretation of scientific inquiry has many supporters, some reject this strong rebuttal to the Enlightenment notion of objectivity in science. The debate over the extent to which reason is historically conditioned in scientific inquiry is not crucial to my position however. For I am concerned with spheres of inquiry that lie outside the boundaries of science.

12. Hans-Georg Gadamer, *Truth and Method*, trans. and ed. Garrett Harden and John Cumming (New York: Seabury Press, 1975), 245–50.

13. Gadamer, *Truth and Method*, 264.

14. The tradition-bound character of moral philosophy has received significant attention in recent years. See, for example, Alisdair MacIntyre, *After Virtue* and *Whose Justice? Which Rationality?* (Notre Dame, Ind.: University of Notre Dame Press, 1988); and Jeffrey Stout, *The Flight from Authority: Religion, Morality and the Quest for Autonomy* (South Bend: University of Notre Dame Press, 1981) and *Ethics After Babel* (Boston: Beacon Press, 1988).

15. Richard John Neuhaus, *The Naked Public Square: Religion and Democracy in America* (Grand Rapids, Mich.: Eerdmans, 1984), 140.

16. Standing within a tradition in one sense necessarily renders that tradition authoritative, oftentimes without awareness of the extent to which the past shapes and constrains the present. Rather than using the term in this weak sense, however, I am attempting to capture the difference between a resource and an authority, the latter granted special privilege in its constraint upon the present.

17. Gadamer, *Truth and Method*, 264.

18. Ibid., 292.

19. For his most recent and complete elaboration of this typology, see *Law's Empire* (Cambridge: Harvard University Press, 1986). Earlier and more concise delineations of this typology can be found in the following: " 'Natural' Law Revisited," *University of Florida Law Review* 34 (1982); and "Law as Interpretation," *Critical Inquiry* 9 (1982).

20. In his earlier articles Dworkin labels the three types of judicial interpretation conventionalism, naturalism, and instrumentalism. In *Law's Empire* he continues to refer to conventionalism but he substitutes "legal pragmatism" for instrumentalism and "law as integrity" for naturalism. His depiction of these forms of judicial interpretation is not substantially different from their formulation in his earlier articles, but his analysis and evaluation of the three types is considerably expanded in *Law's Empire.* I shall largely follow the nomenclature from his earlier writings because these labels are more easily transferable to forms of theological argumentation. However, I will substitute the label "extensionalism" for naturalism because of the misleading associations that may arise for readers of this book between naturalism and the tradition of natural law.

21. Ronald A. Dworkin, " 'Natural' Law Revisited," 178–80. See also *Law's Empire*, 114–50.

22. Dworkin, " 'Natural' Law Revisited," 173; "Law as Interpretation," 195–96. For a more elaborate statement of the interpretive character of all human understanding, see *Law's Empire*, 45–86.

23. Dworkin, "Law as Interpretation," 199.

24. Dworkin, "Law Revisited," 165–66. For Dworkin's very detailed analysis of this second style of judicial interpretation, see *Law's Empire*, 176–275.

25. See, especially, *Law's Empire*, 228–238.

26. Dworkin, "Law Revisited," 160.

27. Dworkin, *Law's Empire*, 227.

28. Ibid.

29. Dworkin, "Law Revisited," 172.

30. Dworkin, *Law's Empire*, 220.

31. Dworkin, "Law Revisited," 181. For a more complete discussion of this style of judicial argumentation, see *Law's Empire*, 151–75.

32. Dworkin, "Law Revisited," 187–88.

33. Ibid., 182–83.

34. Dworkin, *Law's Empire*, 225.

35. Dworkin's penetrating criticisms of the positivistic assumptions of this method are, of course, equally relevant to its theological version. The assumption that past authorities can be mechanically understood and followed, apart from our personal horizons, is untenable.

36. For an argument demonstrating the failure of much Latin American liberation theology to engage in public discourse, through its appeal to an orthopraxis, see Dennis McCann and Charles R. Strain, *Polity and Praxis: A Program for American Practical Theology* (Minneapolis: Winston, 1985). Charles Davis makes a similar criticism of much political theology, contending that it does not reflect an openness to counterarguments which is the mark of public reflection. See *Theology and Political Society* (Cambridge: Cambridge University Press, 1980), 178.

37. Neuhaus, *The Naked Public Square*, 15.

38. Neuhaus, *The Naked Public Square*, 16.

39. Edward Farley, *Ecclesial Reflection: An Anatomy of Theological Method* (Philadelphia: Fortress, 1982).

40. Van A. Harvey, *The Historian and the Believer* (Philadelphia: Westminster, 1966).

41. Gordon Kaufman, *Theology for a Nuclear Age* (Philadelphia: Westminster, 1985), 19.

42. Ibid., 20.

43. The Roman Catholic church, for instance, makes this argument in its "Declaration on the Question of Admission of Women to the Ministerial Priesthood" (Vatican City, October 15, 1976) cited in Rosemary Ruether, *Sexism and God-Talk: Toward a Feminist Theology* (Boston: Beacon Press, 1983), 275.

44. Virginia Mollenkott, "Women and the Bible," in *Mission Trends No. 4: Liberation Theologies*, ed. Gerald Anderson and Thomas Stransky (New York: Paulist, 1979), 222.

45. Mollenkott, "Women and the Bible," 226.

46. Ruether, *Sexism and God-Talk*, 24.

47. Although both Ruether and Mollenkott argue according to the extensionalist theory of interpretation they do not share the same rationale for their approaches. Ruether's appropriation of the past is based upon the need "to assure oneself that one is not mad or duped" or, expressed more positively, the need "to situate oneself meaningfully in history" (*Sexism and God-Talk*, 18). By making the distinction between what in Scripture is for an age and what is for all time, Mollenkott comes close to the conventionalist rationale for basing one's position on the past. That is, she writes as though the Bible is authoritative and hence must inevitably contain specific truths for all time. Despite this assumption, however, her self-conscious procedure in interpreting the Bible falls within the extensionalist framework. The different rationales for their respective uses of the past suggest that these three hermeneutical types exist along a continuum.

48. Elisabeth Schüssler Fiorenza, *In Memory of Her: A Feminist Theological Reconstruction of Christian Origins* (New York: Crossroad, 1983), 56.

49. See, for example, the following works by a philosopher, sociologist, and anthropologist, respectively: Nelson Goodman, *Ways of Worldmaking* (Indianapolis: Hackett, 1978); Peter Berger, *The Sacred Canopy: Elements of a Sociological Theory of Religion* (Garden City: Doubleday/Anchor, 1969); Clifford Geertz, *The Interpretation of Cultures* (New York: Basic Books, 1973). For an argument about the symbolically constructed character of religious experience, see Wayne Proudfoot, *Religious Experience* (Los Angeles: University of California Press, 1985).

50. For the development of this point, see especially Geertz, *The Interpretation of Cultures* (New York: Basic Books, 1973), 89–90.

51. For a similar argument from the perspective of theology, see Schubert Ogden, "Theology and Religious Studies," in *On Theology* (San Francisco: Harper and Row, 1986).

52. Consider for instance feminist thealogians who contend that the symbol of God is hopelessly patriarchal or deconstructive theologians like Mark Taylor who are doing a/theology. Such writings suggest that the genre of theology can no longer be defined in terms of discourse about God.

53. Tracy, *The Analogical Imagination*, 172.

54. George Lindbeck, *The Nature of Doctrine: Religion and Theology in a Postliberal Age* (Philadelphia: Westminster, 1984).

55. Lindbeck, *The Nature of Doctrine*, 21.

56. In *The Interpretation of Otherness: Literature, Religion, and the American Imagination* (New York: Oxford University Press, 1979) Giles Gunn persuasively demonstrates the way in which literature can powerfully alter our visions of reality; see especially 126–74.

57. Michael Walzer, *Interpretation and Social Criticism* (Cambridge: Harvard University Press, 1987), 39.

Chapter 3.

1. For a very helpful historical review of these assumptions, see William M. Sullivan, *Reconstructing Public Philosophy* (Berkeley: University of California Press, 1986), 56–89. For a broader review of individualism within Western culture more generally, see Ralph

Ketcham, *Individualism and Public Life* (New York: Basil Blackwell, 1987), 33–70.

2. The radical inclusivity that characterized the public realm on the theoretical plane was not socially embodied, of course. For the universal dynamic contained within the Enlightenment vision did not operate unimpeded by other constraints. It was refracted through the deeply entrenched structures of domination that were blatantly racist and sexist. Hence, despite the universalism of the Enlightenment rhetoric, which was eventually to prove so important, the initial intention was to preserve the rights and liberties of white, male property owners. From this perspective the purported universalism of the ideology was made possible by relegating those who were not white, male property-owners to the status of "others", not fully human and rational. The moral ramifications of this universal dynamic, then, have been far more ambiguous than they might initially appear.

3. Marx was one of the first to recognize, and criticize, the atomistic individualism at the heart of the eighteenth century liberal vision of self and society. The liberal defense of freedom and rights, he asserted, was of "man regarded as an isolated monad, withdrawn into himself." See Karl Marx, "On the Jewish Question," in *The Marx-Engels Reader*, ed. Robert C. Tucker (New York: Norton, 1978), 42.

4. Burton Bledstein, *The Culture of Professionalism: The Middle Class and the Development of Higher Education in America* (New York: W. W. Norton, 1976). See especially 46–65. For a fascinating account of the process by which a private sphere was carved out from social life, see Philippe Aries, *Centuries of Childhood: A Social History of Family Life*, trans. Robert Baldwick (New York: Alfred A. Knopf, 1962), especially 365–415. Aries contends that it was not until the eighteenth century that a "steadily extending zone of private life," centered in the family, began to isolate itself from society at large (398).

This development has particular significance for the role and status of women. A number of feminist theorists who have pursued issues of gender cross-culturally have noted that the status of women tends to decline as the opposition between the public and domestic spheres increases. For theoretical discussion and historical evidence of this point, see, for instance, *Women and Power in the Middle Ages*, ed. Mary Erler and Maryanne Kowaleski (Athens, Georgia: The University of Georgia Press, 1988). For an excellent analysis of the liberal configuration of public and private through the category of gender, see Zillah Eisenstein, *The Radical Future of Liberal Feminism* (New York: Longman, 1981). Eisenstein clearly shows how the sharp opposition between public and private in the liberal tradition reflects and reinforces patriarchal gender relations and stereotypes. Located within the public world, men have been typically identified in terms of rationality, autonomy, and freedom. Women, on the other hand, have been assimilated to the home and its associated focus on intimacy, relations, nurturing, and dependence. Working women, including most women of color, have long experienced the burdens and tensions of this ideology; although forced to labor in slavery or low wages in the market, they have nonetheless been subject to the norm of domestic femininity and assigned primary responsibility for the home and children as well. The inherent patriarchal structuring of the liberal paradigm of public and private life has become more visible to increasing numbers of women, largely white and middle class, as they too join the work-force and experience first hand the contradictions and costs of simultaneously being "allowed" to enter the public sphere of the market at the same time that they remain primarily identified through and responsible for the private realm. As Eisenstein argues, this development is potentially quite revolutionary as more and more women experience the burdens of being "working mothers," that is, wage-earners who also work a second shift in caring for home and children.

5. The degree to which liberalism obscures the relational dimensions of contemporary life and the degree to which it erodes them are, of course, the subject of much dispute. Michael Walzer's article "The Communitarian Critique of Liberalism" *Political Theory* 18/1 (1990): 6–23 is a very helpful analysis of the two recurring communitarian arguments regarding the relationship between liberal theory and contemporary society: (1) that liberal theory represents society and (2) that liberal theory misrepresents it. He rightly notes that liberal theory does not fully capture contemporary life which clearly includes individuals embedded in various communities and relationships. On the other hand, contemporary society is marked by a high degree of fragmentation and mobility thereby lending much support to the liberal picture. Liberal theory, in my view, functions much like a mythically enhanced caricature of contemporary life. While not a snapshot, its fit is sufficiently close to legitimize it, thereby reinforcing its mythic power to continue shaping society in its own image. The

proposed reconfiguration of public life is an attempt to offer an alternative picture that avoids some of the negative repercussions that flow from the "myth of liberalism" without sacrificing fit entirely.

6. Jean Bethke Elshtain, *Public Man, Private Woman: Women in Social and Political Thought* (Princeton: Princeton University Press, 1981), 184.

7. Parker J. Palmer, *The Company of Strangers: Christians and the Renewal of America's Public Life* (New York: Crossroads, 1982), 36. This book has exerted considerable influence upon my thinking about the substantive agenda of a public theology.

8. Given the interplay between theory and practice, it is equally true that the dramatic social and economic developments of recent centuries have contributed enormously to the emergence and reinforcement of the liberal vision of self and society. Michael Walzer, emphasizing this point, notes that modern life is marked by an unprecedented mobility on the part of its inhabitants, in relation to geography, social status, marriage and family, and political associations. Liberalism is, he suggests, "the theoretical endorsement and justification of this movement." Walzer, "The Communitarian Critique of Liberalism," 12.

9. Palmer, *The Company of Strangers*, 36.

10. Generalizations about twentieth century America focus upon the assumptions and practices that, in terms of numbers and influence, dominate. But American life is not monolithic, and such generalizations inevitably ignore the subcultures that make up the cultural fabric. Thus references to the individualism of contemporary life gloss over the much stronger communal existence more typical of racial and ethnic minorities in this society. In this important respect the portraits of American individualism are exceedingly selective.

11. In her recent work *Rights Talk: The Impoverishment of Political Discourse* (New York: The Free Press, 1991), Mary Ann Glendon reconstructs just such a historical trajectory in American life from the perspective of the legal tradition. She marshals considerable evidence to support her thesis that a new version of rights discourse has emerged in the past thirty years, the distinctiveness of which is reflected in "its starkness and simplicity, its prodigality in bestowing the rights label, its legalistic character,

its exaggerated absoluteness, its hyperindividualism, its insularity, and its silence with respect to personal, civic, and collective responsibilities" (x). Her study sheds considerable light on the characteristics and problems with the prevailing interpretation of public and private life.

12. See, for instance, Robert Bellah et al., *Habits of the Heart* (Berkeley: University of California Press, 1985) and Sullivan, *Reconstructing Public Philosophy*.

13. Cornel West, *Prophetic Fragments* (Grand Rapids, Mich.: William B. Eerdmans Publishing Company, 1988, and Trenton, N.J.: Africa World Press, 1988), 188. In this passage West is citing the work of T. Jackson Lears in *The Culture of Consumption*, ed. Richard Wightman Fox and T. Jackson Lears.

14. For an interesting and accessible account of the emergence of the ethos of consumerism in the American middle class, see Barbara Ehrenreich, *Fear of Falling: The Inner Life of the Middle Class* (New York: Pantheon Books, 1989).

15. Bledstein, *The Culture of Professionalism*, 105.

16. For a useful review of various uses of "community" and "society" as forms of social thought, see Thomas E. McCollough, *The Moral Imagination and Public Life* (Chatham, N.J.: Chatham House Publishers, 1991), 40–51.

17. Jeffrey Stout argues in *Ethics after Babel* (Boston: Beacon, 1988) that we need to move beyond the current impasse between liberalism and communitarianism. He criticizes the former because it "papers over misgivings most of us genuinely feel" and hence reflects a sort of "smug approval of the status quo" (232). At the same time, he criticizes communitarians for the utopian character of their criticism which results merely in a terminal wistfulness. See, especially, 220–42. Michael Walzer, on the other hand, considers communitarianism a recurrent corrective within liberalism. Given the social, economic, and political forces producing the fragmentation in contemporary life, communitarianism, eschewing any triumph over liberalism, must (and should) settle for reinforcing "its internal associative capacities." See "The Communitarian Critique of Liberalism," especially, 21–22.

18. Stout's tactic for moving beyond the impasse of communitarianism and liberalism focuses similarly upon deconstructing the assumption, common to both camps, that diversity ever did go all

the way down in liberal thought or society. By identifying significant areas of mutually shared values, oftentimes ignored because
they reflect a level of platitudinous moral agreement, Stout seeks
to paint a picture of contemporary society for which neither the
liberal label nor the communitarian label is appropriate. See,
especially, *Ethics After Babel*, 233–42. The reconfiguration of public
life proposed herein is based upon a similar strategy of highlighting
features of contemporary life not captured through the prism of
liberalism. However, I am more concerned with the task of mythic
revisioning. Given the growing power of the "myth of liberalism,"
it would seem especially important to engage in mythic reconstruction if the subterranean moral agreement is not only to be
sustained but extended and/or reconfigured in appropriate ways.

19. This point deserves clarification. My concern is to uncover
the grounds that would make us more inclined to recognize a
common life as a prerequisite for the pursuit of our private values
and ends. Commonality in and of itself is not the goal, and I want
to avoid intimating that all commonalities are good. They are often
the product of coercion, or the result of a failure of imagination
or courage as individuals become a clone of their neighbor. It is
not extending commonality, then, that is the goal but securing an
acknowledgement of a common life that qualifies without eliminating our separate pursuits. A common life, then, is not necessarily
a homogeneous life.

20. Some of the more influential thinkers of the nineteenth and
early twentieth century who charted this course include Karl Marx,
G. W. F. Hegel, Emile Durkheim, William James, Josiah Royce, and
George Herbert Mead. More recent exponents are too numerous
to cite, ranging from process philosophers and theologians to
feminist theorists.

21. For a much cited study that develops this argument, see
Michael Sandel, *Liberalism and the Limits of Justice* (Cambridge:
Cambridge University Press, 1982). See also Charles Taylor, *Sources
of the Self: The Making of the Modern Identity* (Cambridge: Harvard
University Press, 1989), especially 25–52.

22. This line of thinking can be traced back to Kant whose
Copernican revolution in philosophy helped to dispel what is
commonly called a naive realism. It is a perspective which, gaining
a historicist twist, animated pragmatic American philosophy at the
turn of the nineteenth century, and which has received contem-

porary expression, for instance, in Richard Rorty's work *Philosophy and the Mirror of Nature* (Princeton: Princeton University Press, 1979).

23. Michael Walzer, "The Communitarian Critique of Liberalism," 14.

24. In another context I have attempted to defend this interpretation of truth more fully, with explicit attention to the challenge that deconstructionism poses. See "Royce and Postmodern Theology," *American Journal of Theology and Philosophy* 9/3 (1988): 149–64.

25. See Stout, *Ethics After Babel*, 210–19.

26. Josiah Royce, *The Problem of Christianity* (Chicago: University of Chicago Press, 1968), 319. Royce's work is devoted in large part to the explanation and defense of the universal community toward which the interpretive process in the search for truth moves. My own thinking about the nature of truth and its relationship to community has been greatly influenced by his writings.

27. Richard Rorty, *Contingency, irony, and solidarity* (New York: Cambridge University Press, 1989), 183.

28. Thomas Levenson, *Ice Time: Climate, Science, and Life on Earth* (New York: Harper and Row, 1989), 91.

29. Thomas Berry, *The Dream of the Earth* (San Francisco: Sierra Club Books, 1988), 42. For other attempts to develop an ecologically sensitive theology, see, for example: John B. Cobb, Jr., and Charles Birch, *The Liberation of Life: From the Cell to the Community* (Cambridge and New York: Cambridge University Press, 1981); Rosemary Ruether, *Sexism and God-Talk: Toward a Feminist Theology* (Boston: Beacon Press, 1983); Sallie McFague, *Models of God: Theology for a Nuclear, Ecological Age* (Philadelphia: Fortress Press, 1987); Jay McDaniel, *Of God and Pelicans: A Theology of Reverence for Life* (Louisville, Ky.: Westminster/John Knox Press, 1989).

30. Michael Walzer, "The Communitarian Critique of Liberalism," 17.

31. Mary Ann Glendon in *Rights Talk* traces the development of legal interpretations of the private sphere, noting the way in which the right to privacy has become interpreted as the "right

188 *Notes*

to be left alone" and assumed the status of a super-trump in legal and public discussions. This interpretation of the right to privacy, she argues, is built upon the faulty anthropology of the solitary individual, the foundation for the sharp separation between the private and the public sphere. As she makes clear, overcoming the sharp separation between these realms does not thereby eliminate the reality or value of a private sphere demanding legal recognition. But it does lead to a reassessment of its character and status, including its role as super-trump in social controversies. See, especially, 47–75.

32. Ronald Dworkin, *Law's Empire* (Cambridge: Harvard University Press, 1986), 190.

33. Clifford Geertz, "The Impact of the Concept of Culture on the Concept of Man," in *The Interpretation of Cultures* (New York: Basic Books, 1973), 52.

34. Will Kymlicka, "Liberalism and Communitarianism," *Canadian Journal of Philosophy* 18/2 (1988): 184.

35. Ibid., 192.

36. Kymlicka is certainly aware of the difference between classical liberalism and its modern variants. He clearly notes that "my concern is with this modern liberalism, not seventeenth-century liberalism, and I want to leave entirely open what the relationship is between the two. It might be that the developments initiated by the 'new liberals' are really an abandonment of what was definitive of classical liberalism." See "Liberalism and Communitarianism," 181. If classical liberalism is recognized as a culturally powerful myth, then the "received wisdom" about it is not a result of ignoring or misreading contemporary philosophical texts.

37. Jeffrey Stout adopts this tactic in *Ethics after Babel*; see, especially, chap. 12.

38. A tradition of "revisionist" moral philosophy has begun to emerge as a challenge to the dominant focus in contemporary ethics upon problems. For an excellent analysis of this slant upon "moral quandaries" in modern ethical literature, see Edmund Pincoffs, "Quandary Ethics," in *Revisions: Changing Perspectives in Moral Philosophy*, ed. Stanley Hauerwas and Alasdair MacIntyre (Notre Dame, Ind.: University of Notre Dame Press, 1983). Those critical of the preoccupation with moral dilemmas typically urge a return

to a focus upon character and the virtues as the central building blocks of the moral life.

39. Hilary Putnam, *The Many Faces of Realism* (LaSalle, Ill.: Open Court, 1987), 51.

40. This is Max Stackhouse's apt depiction of the intertwined worldviews and ethoi to which theology attends.

41. Richard Rorty, *Contingency, irony, and solidarity*, xiii.

42. Ibid., xv.

43. Ibid., xiv.

44. Ibid., xv.

45. This changed view is evident, for instance, in the distance that separates Harvey Cox's 1960s manifesto, *The Secular City: Urbanization and Secularization in Theological Perspective* (New York: Macmillan, 1965) from his more recent work written two decades later, *Religion in the Secular City: Toward a Postmodern Theology* (New York: Simon and Schuster, 1984).

46. Richard C. Martin argues that a form of public theology flourished in medieval Islam before being marginalized and then eclipsed by juridical patterns of religious reflection that reflected a more homogeneous Islamic civilization. He makes this argument in a paper entitled "Public Aspects of Theology in Medieval Islam: The Role of Kalam in Conflict Definition and Resolution," which was delivered in July 1991 at the international conference "Approaches to the Study of Islam," held at the University of Capetown in South Africa. The conference papers are currently being prepared for publication.

47. Gordon D. Kaufman, *God the Problem* (Cambridge: Harvard University Press, 1972), 100.

Chapter 4.

1. To prevent misunderstanding, I should note that my use of the term 'ontology' does not presume access to the nature of being as it is in itself, that is, unaffected by the historical and cultural location of the interpreter. Ontologies constitute interpretations of the nature of being and ultimate reality which are profoundly shaped by the traditions operative in a particular place and time.

2. H. Richard Niebuhr, *Radical Monotheism and Western Culture* (New York: Harper and Row, 1943), 32.

3. Behind these observations looms the critical problem of religious pluralism. It is a multifaceted problem that cannot be adequately treated in this work. Nevertheless, I would like to identify the orientation, as I see it, of a public theology on this issue, particularly given the misleading impression that might arise from the preceding remarks. The respect for "the other" that monotheism engenders should not be taken to mean that monotheism cultivates an indifference to questions of truth by allowing "every flower to bloom" out of respect for its divine source. Our choices are not between an absolutism based upon divine revelation or a radical relativism based upon equal toleration of all views. The creation symbolism does not provide much help here, for its static character fails to take account of the processes through which truth is pursued. I would argue that the engagement with the various world religions should proceed in much the same fashion as the pursuit of truth within a single tradition. Neither absolutism nor relativism captures the process through which traditions endure and develop through the centuries in response to evolving contexts that include new discoveries, different problems, and new and changed conversation partners. The contemporary situation is distinctive insofar as it has made both possible and necessary a far more extensive conversation among the various religions. But the process by which Christians engage in dialogue with Buddhists, for example, is akin to the earlier and fateful conversation between early Christianity and Greek philosophy. For a very illuminating historical account of the interaction and development of traditions see Alisdair MacIntyre's exploration of modern philosophy in *Whose Justice? Which Rationality?* (Notre Dame, Ind.: University of Notre Dame Press, 1988). John B. Cobb illustrates and defends a similar construal of continuity and change in traditions from a theological perspective in *Beyond Dialogue: Toward a Mutual Transformation of Christianity and Buddhism* (Philadelphia: Fortress Press, 1982).

4. Recognizing this point, Christian theologians, including Jonathan Edwards and Karl Barth, have often noted that the various roles humans attribute to God are in fact one, their distinction a function of the human perspective from which God is interpreted.

5. Perhaps more than any other contemporary theologian, James M. Gustafson has developed and defended an interpretation

of God in terms of the natural ordering processes in creation. See, especially, *Ethics from a Theocentric Perspective: Theology and Ethics* (Chicago: University of Chicago Press, 1981).

6. Wayne Proudfoot analyzes the characteristics of and motivation behind this apologetic strategy in *Religious Experience* (Berkeley: University of California Press, 1985).

7. Ian G. Barbour, *Religion in an Age of Science* (San Francisco: Harper Collins Publishers, 1990), 16.

8. The most sustained efforts to work out a reapprochement between religion and science in the twentieth century have been pursued by process theologians who have been especially influenced by Alfred North Whitehead and Charles Hartshorne. For other contributions to this dialogue see, for example, Ian G. Barbour, *Religion in an Age of Science*; Charles Birch and John Cobb, Jr., *The Liberation of Life: From the Cell to the Community* (Cambridge: Cambridge University Press, 1981); David Ray Griffin, ed., *The Reenchantment of Science: Postmodern Proposals* (Albany: SUNY Press, 1988); Ernan McMullin, ed., *Evolution and Creation* (Notre Dame, Ind.: University of Notre Dame Press, 1985); Ted Peters, ed., *Cosmos as Creation: Theology and Science in Consonance* (Nashville: Abingdon Press, 1989); Arthur Peacocke, *Creation and the World of Science* (Oxford: Clarendon Press, 1979); Idem, *God and the New Biology* (San Francisco: Harper and Row, 1986).

9. John Polkinghorne, *Science and Creation: The Search for Understanding* (Bristol, England: SPCK, 1988), 67.

10. This is not to deny that spiritual and psychological sustenance can be gained by affirming that atonement is possible and will be acceptable and pleasing to God. But as James Cone has persuasively argued, the modern propensity to emphasize God's love to the exclusion of God's wrath lends religious legitimation to the myriad forms of oppression that constitute social life. See, for example, James Cone, *A Black Theology of Liberation* (Maryknoll, N.Y.: Orbis, 1986).

11. Josiah Royce has developed one of the most powerful modern expressions of this understanding of atonement in *The Problem of Christianity* (Chicago: University of Chicago Press, 1968).

12. H. Richard Niebuhr, *Faith on Earth: An Inquiry into the Structure of Human Faith*, ed. Richard R. Niebuhr (New Haven: Yale University Press, 1989), 117.

13. For a discussion of these propensities see, for example, Carol Christ, "Yahweh as Holy Warrior," in *Laughter of Aphrodite: Reflections on a Journey to the Goddess* (San Francisco: Harper & Row, 1987); Catherine Keller, *From a Broken Web: Separation, Sexism, and Self* (Boston: Beacon Press, 1986); and Susan Brooks Thistlethwaite, " 'I Am Become Death': God in the Nuclear Age," in *Lift Every Voice: Constructing Christian Theologies from the Underside*, ed. Susan Brooks Thistlethwaite and Mary Potter Engel (San Francisco: Harper & Row, 1990).

14. Sallie McFague in *Models of God*, for instance, develops the metaphor of the world as God's body in an effort to overcome the devaluation of women, nature, and the body in traditional theism.

15. Rachel Adler, "A Question of Boundaries: Toward a Jewish Feminist Theology of Self and Others," *Tikkun* 6/3 (1991): 45.

16. Ibid.

Chapter 5.

1. Joan C. Callahan, *Ethical Issues in Professional Life* (New York: Oxford University Press, 1988), 26–27.

2. Burton J. Bledstein persuasively develops this line of argument in his fascinating study *The Culture of Professionalism: The Middle Class and the Development of Higher Education in America* (New York: W. W. Norton and Company, Inc., 1976). For a similar analysis focusing on the past three decades within American society, see Barbara Ehrenreich, *Fear of Falling* (New York: Pantheon Books, 1989).

3. Studies that I have found helpful in providing historical perspective on the relationship between theology and professionalization include: Yves M. J. Congar, O.P. *A History of Theology*, trans. and ed. Hunter Guthrie, S.J. (Garden City, N.Y.: Doubleday and Company, 1968); Edward Farley, *Theologia: The Fragmentation and Unity of Theological Education* (Philadelphia: Fortress Press, 1983), especially 29–48; G. R. Evans, *Old Arts and New Theology* (Oxford: Clarendon Press, 1980); and Lowrie J. Daly, S.J., *The Medieval University 1200–1400* (New York: Sheed and Ward, 1961).

4. G. R. Evans, *Old Arts and New Theology*, 28–29.

5. Yves Congar, *A History of Theology*, 166.

6. Miriam Usher Chrisman, *Lay Culture, Learned Culture, 1450–1599* (New Haven: Yale University Press, 1982), xx–xxi. Chrisman carefully reconstructs the intellectual and social life of the city of Strasbourg during the sixteenth century through a study of the writers, publishers, and readers of the texts that were published during this period. Her study sheds considerable light on the intersection between genre, style, and audience in the Reformation.

7. For a very informative summary of some of the critical intellectual and social effects of the invention of the printing press on Western culture, see Elizabeth L. Eisenstein, "Some Conjectures about the Impact of Printing on Western Society: A Preliminary Report," *Journal of Modern History* 40 (1968); her later, more extensive study of this phenomena was published as *The Printing Press as an Agent of Change*, vols. 1 and 2, (Cambridge: Cambridge University Press, 1979).

8. Cited in Bledstein, *The Culture of Professionalism*, 277.

9. Bruce Kuklick, *The Rise of American Philosophy: Cambridge, Massachusetts, 1860–1930* (New Haven: Yale University Press, 1977), 565. Kuklick's book is a comprehensive account of the causes and effects of the professionalization of higher education as viewed through the changes in the Department of Philosophy at Harvard University between 1860 and 1930.

10. Edward Farley, *The Fragility of Knowledge: Theological Education in the Church and the University* (Philadelphia: Fortress Press, 1988), 39. Farley devotes an entire chapter of this work to exploring the nature and problematic repercussions of specialization in the modern university. See 29–55. See also the general critique of academic disciplines in Herman E. Daly and John B. Cobb, Jr., *For the Common Good: Redirecting the Economy Toward Community, the Environment, and a Sustainable Future* (Boston, Beacon Press, 1989), especially 25–43, 121–37.

11. Cornel West, *The American Evasion of Philosophy: A Genealogy of Pragmatism* (Madison, Wis.: University of Wisconsin Press, 1989), 3.

12. Bledstein, *The Culture of Professionalism*, 90.

13. Bledstein, *The Culture of Professionalism*, 14–15.

14. This generalization is somewhat misleading in regard to the formation of women's identity. To the extent that women's

identity has remained more relationally constituted, the generalization is rooted in the experience of middle-class men, and, only more recently, increasing numbers of middle-class women. On the other hand, insofar as a woman's identity is a function of the status and achievement of a significant male "other," the generalization applies to women as well, if less directly.

15. Bruce Wilshire, *The Moral Collapse of the University: Professionalism, Purity, and Alienation* (Albany: State University of New York Press, 1989), x–xiii.

16. George Lindbeck, *The Nature of Doctrine: Religion and Theology in a Postliberal Age* (Philadelphia: Westminster, 1984), 84.

17. Lindbeck, *The Nature of Doctrine*, 118.

18. Wayne Proudfoot, *"Regulae fidei* and Regulative Idea: Two Contemporary Theological Strategies" in *Theology at the End of Modernity*, ed. Sheila Greeve Davaney (Philadelphia: Trinity Press International, 1991), 112.

19. Some postmodern narrative theologies grant more room and importance to conversations between the tradition and the culture at large. William Placher, for instance, in *Unapologetic Theology: A Christian Voice in a Pluralistic Conversation* (Louisville, Ky.: Westminster/John Knox Press, 1989) represents this strand within narrative theology.

20. David Tracy, *The Analogical Imagination: Christian Theology and the Culture of Pluralism* (New York: Crossroad, 1981), 57.

21. Ibid.

22. Ibid.

23. Ibid.

24. See, for example, Delwin Brown, "Thinking about the God of the Poor," *Journal of the American Academy of Religion* 57 (1989): 267–81.

25. Tracy, *The Analogical Imagination*, 6.

26. Ibid., 26.

27. Consider, for example, Katie Geneva Cannon's interpretation of the meaning and role of Christianity in the African-American experience which challenges many of the "essentialist"

feminist critiques of Christian symbols typically written from the perspective of white women. For a development of her argument, see "The Emergence of Black Feminist Consciousness," in Letty M. Russell, ed., *Feminist Interpretation of the Bible* (Philadelphia: Westminster Press, 1985). See also Katie G. Cannon, *Black Womanist Ethics* (Atlanta, Ga.: Scholars Press, 1988) and Susan B. Thistlethwaite, *Sex, Race, and God: Christian Feminism in Black and White* (New York: Crossroad, 1989).

28. The recognition of the multiplicity of chapters within the tradition that cannot be harmonized or unified into a coherent novel raises questions about the cogency of the metaphor itself. As I see it, the adequacy of the metaphor depends upon whether one is assuming a theological or a historical perspective. A historian sees multiplicity and describes it. A theologian also sees multiplicity but seeks to distill the most compelling trajectory in order to extend the tradition. As Ernst Troeltsch explained when wrestling with a similar problem, the interpretation of the essence of Christianity is as much a normative endeavor as a descriptive one.

29. The development in Gordon Kaufman's theology, in my view, reflects this trajectory. In *Theology for a Nuclear Age* he pays less attention to the logical features of the concept of God and concentrates more on beliefs and behaviors connected with notions of divine power and eschatology that are operative in the wider culture. I have developed this interpretation of his work in "Resisting the Postmodern Turn: Theology and Contextualization," in *Theology at the End of Modernity*, 81–98.

Chapter 6.

1. It would be misleading to suggest without qualification that the liberal tradition from its inception has endorsed such a utilitarian conception of personhood. An important early strand of liberalism construed the individual as in some sense sacred, providing the rationale, for example, for Kant's principle of respect for persons, or the concern for individual rights within modern western political and legal theory. This interpretation of the individual has been increasingly eclipsed in the liberal tradition, however, as bureaucratic and utilitarian influences have grown stronger.

2. Thomas E. McCollough, *The Moral Imagination and Public Life* (Chatham, N.J.: Chatham House Publishers, Inc., 1991), 80.

3. Robert B. Reich. "Secession of the Successful," *The New York Times Magazine*, (January 20, 1991): 42. See also Robert B. Reich, *The Work of Nations: Preparing Ourselves for 21st Century Capitalism* (New York: Alfred A. Knopf, 1991), 277–78.

4. Reich, "Secession of the Successful", 42.

5. Barbara Ehrenreich, *Fear of Falling: The Inner Life of the Middle Class* (New York: Pantheon Books, 1989), 249.

6. Bellah makes this point in an interview with Bill Moyers. See Bill Moyers, *A World of Ideas* (New York: Doubleday, 1989), 287.

7. Robert B. Reich, *Tales of a New America* (New York: Times Books, 1987), 50.

8. For an analysis of the way in which this understanding of politics shapes citizenship, leadership, and decision-making in contemporary America, see Ralph Ketcham, *Individualism and Public Life* (New York: Basic Blackwell, 1987), 134–219.

9. Meg Greenfield, "Nationalizing Their Pitch," *Newsweek* (August 5, 1991): 66.

10. Robert Reich persuasively demonstrates the way in which American assumptions concerning governmental programs reflect and exacerbate a loss of national solidarity. We regard social insurance programs as legitimate ways of ensuring "us" against future hardship; the logic underscores our interdependence and emphasizes that we are all in this together. Welfare, on the other hand, is construed as charity to "them" and the accent is on the difference between "us" and "them". In tight economic times this logic is especially fatal to "them." See Reich, *Tales of a New America*, 155–76.

11. Charles Davis's distinction between the private self and the interior self clarifies this point. The private self, spawned by modernity's configuration of the public and private realms, is inadequate in two related but distinguishable ways. First, social and political affairs are considered peripheral to the concerns of the private self; secondly, the private self is thought to be constituted apart from the influences of the social and political spheres. As Davis makes clear, however, rejecting the privatized self is not the same as rejecting the interior self, that individual self–awareness at the heart of human freedom and responsibility. This interior self, which Davis construes as a mystical core opening

toward a transcendent horizon, is critical to preventing public life from turning into a totalitarian or bureaucratic system in which the individual is radically devalued. See *What Is Living, What Is Dead in Christianity Today?: Breaking the Liberal-Conservative Deadlock* (San Francisco: Harper and Row, Publishers, 1986). See, especially, 96–105.

12. H. Richard Niebuhr, "Faith in Gods and in God," in *Radical Monotheism and Western Culture* (New York: Harper and Row, 1970), 126.

13. Charles Davis, *Theology and Political Society* (Cambridge: Cambridge University Press, 1980), 169.

14. William C. Placher, *Unapologetic Theology: A Christian Voice in a Pluralistic Conversation* (Louisville, Ky.: Westminster/ John Knox Press, 1989), 160.

15. Burton Mack develops the categories of the caretaker and critic of religion in a paper entitled "Caretakers and Critics: On the Social Role of Scholars Who Study Religion," which he delivered at Arizona State University in November 1989. He argues persuasively that the prevailing role of scholars of religion toward their subject has been largely, and inappropriately, that of caretaker.

16. Edward Farley, *The Fragility of Knowledge: Theological Education in the Church and the University* (Philadelphia: Fortress Press, 1988), 70.

17. Cited in an interview with Bill Moyers in *A World of Ideas*, 459.

18. In other writings I have adopted a more historical approach to the topic of public theology by developing it in and through an exploration of the writings of Josiah Royce, H. Richard Niebuhr, and Gordon Kaufman, three key figures in the evolution of this tradition of American religious reflection. See, especially, "A Model For a Public Theology," *Harvard Theological Review* 80 (1987) and "The Task of a Public Theology" in Ronald F. Thiemann, ed., *The Legacy of H. Richard Niebuhr* (Philadelphia: Fortress Press, 1991).

19. Max Stackhouse has attempted to trace the historical roots of this form of American public theology in his work *Public Theology and Political Economy* (Grand Rapids, Mich.: Eerdmans, 1987). See 36–92.

20. H. Richard Niebuhr, *Radical Monotheism and Western Culture*, 62.

Index

Adler, Rachel, 117
Arendt, Hannah, 15, 172n11
Aries, Philippe, 182n4
Augustine, 123

Barbour, Ian, 107
Barth, Karl, 190n4
Bell, Daniel, 17
Bellah, Robert, 2, 21–23, 70, 153
Bible: contrasted with U.S.
  Constitution, 61–62; creation
  in, 101; patriarchy as cultural
  background for, 52–53, 143; role
  in extensionalist theology of,
  135, 180n47; theology as
  interpretation of, 24, 50, 122
Bledstein, Burton, 70–71, 129,
  130

Cannon, Katie G., 194–95n27
Cassirer, Ernst, 57
Chrisman, Miriam V., 193n6
Christianity: the Bible and, 132–33;
  Christocentry of, 116; early
  theology of, 49–50, 122–123;
  reconfiguration of public life and,
  94; reflection in, 24–25; role in
  American life of, 19, 21–22;
  unifying element of, 132–33.
  See also Bible; God; Jesus
Coleman, John, 168
Common good, 73–74, 88–89
Common life: anthropocentric
  interpretation of, 82; bases of,
  74–75; definition of, 73;

distinguished from common
  good, 73–74, 88; monotheism
  and, 110; need for more
  inclusive meaning of, 81–84;
  pursuit of truth and, 80;
  theology and, 92. See also
  Public life
Communitarianism, 72–73, 151–52,
  183–84n5, 185–86n17–18
Cone, James, 114
Conventionalism: in jurisprudence,
  42–43, 44, 47; in theology,
  48–51
Creation, 101

Daly, Mary, 114
Davis, Charles, 160–61, 179n36,
  196–97n11
Delattre, Roland, 17
Democracy, communal focus of, 2
Dewey, John, 14, 15
Dworkin, Ronald A., 41–45,
  46–48, 86, 87, 178n20

Edwards, Jonathan, 190n4
Eisenstein, Zillah, 182–83n4
Eliade, Mircea, 58
Elshtain, Jean B., 172n10
Enlightenment: ideal of objectivity,
  36, 37, 38; interpretation of
  public, 16, 66–68; privatization
  of religion, 9–10; role of science,
  128–29; view of reason, 11–12,
  13, 37. See also Liberalism,
  philosophical

199

Otto, Rudolph, 58

Placher, William, 164
Polkinghorne, John, 107
Private life/sphere, 6–8, 13–14,
  68, 148–51
Professionalism: in America,
  125–31; culture of, 120;
  ideology of, 128–30; in theology,
  120–24
Proudfoot, Wayne, 133
Public: ahistorical interpretation
  of, 33; as community of persons,
  16; discourse, 119–20; meanings
  of, 34–35, 36; virtue, 18, 19. See
  also Common life; Public life;
  Theology, public
Public life/sphere: in America,
  7–8, 154–57; as common life,
  14–15, 89–90, 152–53;
  definition of, 6; eclipse of,
  15–16; Enlightenment roots of,
  66; escape from, 14; global, 73,
  153–54; God and, 163; Greek,
  6–7; importance of individual
  in, 85–86, 158; monotheism and
  reinterpretation of, 98–99,
  117–18; morality and, 20–21;
  private life contrasted with,
  148–51; radical individualism
  of, 67–68, 70–71; receptacle
  model of, 68–69; reconfiguration
  of, 84–87. See also Common
  life; Theology, public
Putnam, Hilary, 90

Rauschenbusch, Walter, 168
Rawls, John, 88
Reason: contextual nature of,
  35–36, 38–39; Enlightenment
  view of, 11–12, 13, 37; means
  vs. ends and, 12
Reformation, 9
Reich, Robert B., 151, 153, 157,
  175n48, 196n10

Religion: civil, 21–23; conflict
  with science of, 100–101, 107;
  exclusion from public life of,
  20–21; as learned experience,
  59, 60; "New Age", 71; in
  nineteenth century America,
  19; privatization of, 1–4, 9–10,
  20; public, 3, 4, 5, 23, 24;
  theology and, 24, 25; in
  university curriculum, 165–67;
  vitality of, 92–93. See also
  Monotheism; Theology;
  Theology, public
Religious pluralism, 190n3
Rorty, Richard, 80, 90–91
Royce, Josiah, 14, 168, 187n26
Ruether, Rosemary, 53, 168,
  180n47

Sandel, Michael, 88
Schüssler Fiorenza, Elisabeth,
  54–55, 143
Science: objectivity in, 177n11;
  religion and, 100–101, 107
Self, 75–77, 85, 129–30,
  196–97n11. See also Identity
Sennett, Richard, 13–14
Sin, 108–9
Specialization, in modern
  university, 125–28
Stackhouse, Max, 3
Stout, Jeffrey, 185n17, 185–86n18
Sullivan, William, 11, 12, 18, 70

Theology: authoritarian mode of,
  24–25, 176n53; as biblical
  commentary, 122–23, 142;
  common life and, 92;
  conventionalism in, 48–51;
  development, as academic
  discipline of, 123–24; extensionalism in, 51–56, 63, 64, 135;
  feminist, 52–55; function of,
  56–64; fundamental, 34–35,
  136–37; instrumentalism in,